AWARE
of the Ultimate Reality

J. R. MORRIS

Copyright © 2019 J. R. Morris
All rights reserved
First Edition

PAGE PUBLISHING, INC.
New York, NY

First originally published by Page Publishing, Inc. 2019

ISBN 978-1-68456-158-2 (Paperback)
ISBN 978-1-64544-623-1 (Hardcover)
ISBN 978-1-68456-159-9 (Digital)

Printed in the United States of America

To my precious wife, siblings, children, and the memory
of my mother and father.

And of course, to God
and all those who abide with Him.

Contents

Introduction 7

I. Early Years 9
1. Near-Death Experiences 9
2. TV Failure at Ten Years of Age.............................10
3. A Broken Leg 11
4. Physics Books 13
5. A Submarine Model 14

II. Miracles.. 15
6. Lourdes, France 15
7. My Neck Injury..17
8. Funerals..18
9. A Friend's Bout with Cancer 20
10. My Stepson's Attention-Deficit Disorder (ADD)....................21

III. Direct Interventions 23
11. My Son's Hip Problem 23
12. A Promotion, a Skiing Trip, and a Divorce 25
13. Cancer Diagnosis and the Voice 29
14. My Father's Illness and the Voice 30
15. The Evil One..31
16. God's Intervention with Two Homes 36

IV. Divine Interactions 38
17. Fatima, Portugal 38
18. The Wheat and Weeds Parable 39
19. Malachi 41
20. Interactions with My Deceased Stepfather and Mother 42

21. Precious Moments with Children 45
22. Precious Moments with Animals 49
23. Other Interactions 53

V. Asks **66**
24. Asks for a Son 66
25. World Leader Requests 68
26. Other Asks 69
27. Ask Summary 79

VI. Jesus **81**
28. A Sad Newspaper Article 81
29. Direct Interactions with Jesus 83
30. Acquaintance Experiences 85
31. Was Jesus Married? 87

VII. Precognitions **90**
32. A Prophecy 90
33. Direct Precognitions 91
34. Other Precognitive Events 93
35. What Is Precognition? 96

VIII. Intuition **97**
36. Work Experiences 97
37. Opportunities Missed 100
38. A Glimpse of the Hereafter from Science? 103
39. What Is Intuition? 104

IX. This Book **106**
40. Why Write the Book? 106
41. Distractions 108
42. An Ask Answered 111
43. Wave of a Hand 111
44. The Rule of Thirds? 112

X. Final Remarks **113**

Attachment 1 117

Introduction

This book seeks to answer the question "Is there an ultimate reality beyond our directly observable, four-dimensional space-time continuum?" Is it logical, rational, or even prudent to think there might be something else? Why would we even question the existence of anything beyond what we can directly observe and measure? Is there any way to experience or know anything else?

My true-life experiences, summarized in this book, prove to me there is an ultimate reality—one we all experience and interact with whether we are conscious of it or not. Hopefully, this book will give you, the reader, a sense of how to become aware of the ultimate reality. My experiences and those of a few acquaintances are only a guide for you. Because of free will, your level of awareness is up to you. Hopefully, you will analyze your past and future life experiences with an open mind. Experiment. Ask the monotheistic God to help you, your family, and acquaintances often. Teach your children from day one by example. If you're not already aware of God's and Satan's existence, analyze your motives and feelings before and after your experiences—you will learn why being aware is so important. Learn the benefits of asking, forgiving, being compassionate, and experiencing God's love (agape love).

Your degree of awareness will depend on your own unique life experiences, circumstances, personality, culture, and state-of-grace (how close you are to God at any one moment). It is my judgment while my specific awareness experiences are unique to me, my conclusions are universal. They apply to all humanity.

As to my specific experiences, I have been married to my present wife for twenty years. I enjoy the time I have been able to spend with my stepdaughter and my two sons from a previous marriage. I truly loved and miss my two stepchildren from a second marriage. Many of my family experiences include direct interactions with the ultimate reality and are included in this book.

I

Early Years

The Helping Hand I Did Not See

1. Near-Death Experiences

When I was three years old, I was hospitalized with pneumonia for a week. Without penicillin, which had become available only three years earlier, I would have died. When I was nine, I fell ten feet out of a tree, fracturing the left side of my head on a cone-shaped rock. The babysitter called my parents and let them talk to me. I told my parents the hero on one of my favorite TV shows was killed. My parents came home and rushed me to the hospital, where two neurologists reviewed the x-rays and determined I did not need surgery. I was hospitalized for a week in the hospital before I regained consciousness and could even remember climbing the tree. Later that year, I tried climbing a twelve-foot bank on my bike and fell into a broken milk bottle, cutting my right wrist. Since I could see blood squirting with every heartbeat, I held my wrist tightly until I could get home. My father, being a World War II medic, held a pressure point near my shoulder until he could get me to the hospital. If my father had not been home or anything else had gone differently, I might have bled to death. Any one of these three experiences had a probability of causing death. In retrospect, I am lucky to have survived my early childhood. Did I have a guardian angel looking out for me? I think so.

2. TV Failure at Ten Years of Age

When my mother was registering me for the fifth grade, the school district wanted to hold me back one year in school. My reading level was fourth grade first month. My mother refused and registered me in the fifth grade. Being an English and history teacher, she knew what to do. For the better part of a year, she unplugged the TV and told me it was broken. I never checked—it's a good thing I trusted my mother. We lived high in the Rocky Mountains in a small house. My bedroom was in an uninsulated attic, and I had to do my homework there. My mother gave me two books to read that she had read when she was my age. With nothing else to do at night but homework and read, my grades went up significantly. I started reading abridged books and quickly found myself reading anything I could get my hands on—including my father's western book collection. Occasionally, my mother would ask what I was reading. Once, I told her I had started reading *A Tale of Two Cities* (only the first one hundred pages) but found it boring. I told her the first line was interesting: "It was the best of times. It was the worst of times." My judgment now? It applies to all "times." I then told my mother I had completed *The Leatherstocking Tales* and several other novels, short stories, and poems, including some written by Edgar Allen Poe. My fifth-grade teacher would quiz me on each book and, if I answered correctly, place a star decal on the class reading chart. I quickly got to the maximum of fifty-two stars but continued to read every night. My reading level went from 4.1 to 9.8 in one year. My grades had improved with fifteen As and one B—penmanship (yes, my penmanship is still so poor; often I still can't read it). My mother had effectively changed my life. Because of this one year's experience, I knew how to study, eventually going to five universities, obtaining three degrees, and earning membership in a national honor society. Parental actions really do have a dramatic effect on their children's future. If you do nothing else in life, love children and help them learn.

During the fifth grade, I had a curious experience on a geography test. I missed one question: "Where are the Juan de Fuca

Straits?" I had no idea. So I looked it up on a United States map. I find it curious I have lived most of my adult life within sight of those straits. Was this just coincidence? I think not.

3. A Broken Leg

When I was twelve, I experienced the most painful and loudest of God's interventions in my life so far. Though I didn't know it at the time, the experience would change my life forever. I broke my leg during a school gym-class tumbling accident. The physical education teacher had rolled two tumbling mats together with the intent of having us run and do a handspring over both mats, landing on a third flat mat. I was standing way back in line. All the other boys in front of me were too scared to attempt the stunt. Being the smallest, I was pushed to the front of the line. I thought, *Better to get it over with*, so I ran toward the rolled-up mats as fast as I could. As I remember, the handspring went rather well. I went over the top and landed perpendicular to the flat mat and continued into a forward roll. I landed hard. The tread on my new tennis shoes were very deep, acting like suction cups. The landing mat was nonporous. Most of my weight was on my right leg. The result? My right leg stuck to the mat long enough to cause a four-inch oblique break in my right tibia. My leg felt like it was on fire. The PE instructor wanted me to get up and try to walk. I refused. If I had done so, the consequences could have been disastrous. My parents came to the school and took me to a hospital where my leg was put into a cast. Because it wasn't set, it ached for many years with changes in humidity. I was in a cast for several months.

The public junior high I attended prior to breaking my leg had no elevators to the second and third floors where most of my classes were held. So I had to go up and down heavily trafficked stairs on crutches to get from one class to another. The situation was untenable. My crutches were frequently taken as a prank. Once, I had a knife thrown between my legs.

My parents pulled me out of the public school and enrolled me in the local one-story parochial school. Though my mother was Catholic, our family didn't practice any one religion. As a family, we had attended several different Protestant churches, but I had never been inside a Catholic church. I was very apprehensive. Previously, when we had lived close to the parochial school, I used to get into rock fights with the school's older boys. Every morning before school I had to attend something called mass. I also had to attend catechism classes with the school's monsignor twice a week. I was in for a very different school experience. But there was no alternative. Looking back, I suspect God had a hand in this experience.

The first morning, my father took me to meet Mother Superior, my new teacher. Unlike the public school, she taught most subjects, so I didn't have to change classrooms all the time. Mother Superior seemed pleasant, but her clothing was certainly different. After introductions, Mother Superior asked a passing girl to take me to our classroom. She was very polite (and very cute). Once settled at my desk, I noticed all the students were in their seats before the bell rang—something I had never seen before. Shortly after the bell, Mother Superior entered the room. All the students instantly stopped talking and stood up. Another first for me. I didn't know what to do. I couldn't get up fast enough. As she approached her desk, Mother Superior motioned for me to stay in my seat. After Mother Superior and the students exchanged greetings, we started into the first lesson—the story of Mother Seton (never heard of her before). She has since been canonized a saint.

The students in this new school were pleasant and respectful to each other and, especially, to their teachers. No unannounced police raids to check lockers for weapons, drugs, and dynamite (yep, they found wet, unstable dynamite in the public junior high school lockers). No more being led out of classrooms into hallways and frisked. And in the new school, learn we did.

Early one very cold morning, I was the first student in church. When I sat down, I was so warm I took off my coat, gloves, and hat. I was still comfortably warm. I spent my time studying the church altar, windows, statues, and wood pews. The church smelled grand—very inviting. I couldn't kneel yet, but that would come in time. When the rest of the students came in, they all left their warm clothes on, complaining about how cold the church was—no one had turned on the heater. In the town where we lived, it could snow any time of the year—even in July. Over the many months I spent at that school, I don't ever remember being cold in that church. A miracle? In retrospect, highly likely. Today, I am certain I was where I was supposed to be!

After another year in the Rocky Mountains, my family moved to Carmel, California. My brother and I attended the Carmel Mission parochial school where I was confirmed. Near the end of my first confession, the priest said, "You and God are very close." I am still not sure what prompted the comment; maybe he said that to all of us eighth graders. Still, it seemed like a good thing to know.

Why have I spent so much time on these experiences? I don't think I would ever have been aware of the ultimate reality if I hadn't broken my leg. And without Jesus, there would have been no church or school to attend. Does God use pain and suffering to redirect and focus our lives? I think so. People who are not aware of having experienced subtle (and sometimes not so subtle), direct God interventions in their lives are at risk of living in a void. When anyone experiences a direct God intervention and eventually recognizes it as such, spirituality is no longer just a hope or belief—one knows there is an ultimate reality.

4. Physics Books

When I was thirteen, my parents took my brother and me on a shopping trip to San Francisco. When we got there, our parents gave each of us fifteen dollars to spend as we wanted. But we had to be back in the car in three hours. I was compelled to go immediately to a bookstore. I was drawn to two books. If I remember correctly, one was titled *The Universe and Albert Einstein*, and the other, *One Two Three…Infinity* by George Gamow, is still in print. I went back to the car and started to read. Hours later, my family returned and asked what I bought. I told them I bought a physics book and a math book and started to read both. I asked my mother if she knew about the Schrodinger equation and the Hertzberg uncertainty principle. She said no. So I tried to explain the significance of each. Then I announced that I wanted to be a physicist. My mother said that I wasn't smart enough to be a physicist—it was the toughest subject in college. I thought to myself, *We'll see about that!* And I never questioned again what I was going to be. Many decades later when I applied for and got the position of head of Research and Technology Development at a major university physics laboratory, guess who the first person I called? My mother, of course. To this day, I think her negative comment helped me resolve to become a physicist.

5. A Submarine Model

When I was seventeen, I spent the summer with my grandparents while my mother moved the family to her new job. During the days, I worked at a service station. At night, I assembled a model of the George Washington Subsurface Ship Ballistic Nuclear (SSBN) submarine. I became aware of its compartments including interconnecting bulkhead power, electrical, and steam systems. Interestingly, four years later, after I graduated from college, my first position was assisting on overhaul planning for Polaris and Poseidon submarines. In retrospect, working on the SSBN model doesn't seem like coincidence. I worked on undersea weapon systems based near the Juan de Fuca Straits as an engineering physicist for twenty-plus years. My classified defense department positions, plus being married with two children, kept me from being drafted into the Vietnam War. Another direct God intervention?

In retrospect, surviving childhood, my parents' focus on education, and my interests, hobbies, and professional career all seem synchronized by the presence of a higher power. Was His long-term objective for me to help raise four pairs of sibling children and write this book on awareness of His presence in all our lives? I think so.

II

Miracles

*Some are very loud, some are small,
some seem less direct, but all justify my faith.*

6. Lourdes, France

When I was young, my mother was seeking meaning in her life, awareness if you will. She met a lady from a different Christian religion—Catholic. The lady told her about an experience she had at Lourdes, France. Before the lady's trip to Europe, she had been scheduled for cataract surgery upon her return. At Lourdes, she went into the baths. When the lady returned home, her cataract surgeon told her she did not have any signs of cataracts. The lady's conclusion? She had experienced a miracle. I never forgot this story.

Many decades later, my wife and I joined a bus tour of Europe. I was particularly intrigued with the opportunity to visit the place called Lourdes. For two years before the trip, I suffered a severe ache in my right leg—it kept me awake almost every night. The x-rays and ultrasound tests did not reveal the cause. At a doctor's suggestion, I was taking naproxen sodium pills—sometimes twice a day. I was particularly concerned I would lose sleep during our Europe trip, so I increased the dose to four pills a day, two in the morning and two at night. I still had an ache in my right leg but was able to function.

Early on the second day of our Lourdes tour, my wife woke me saying the tour guide wanted to leave immediately. I got up and quickly dressed, forgetting both my pills and a warm sweater—I had lost my coat two days earlier. Located at the northern foot of the Pyrenees, Lourdes is cold in October. During the day's tour, those of us who chose to entered the baths. For no reason other than my mother's story, I quickly lined up and entered with the first group. I was the first from the group to enter the bath. After removing my outer layer of clothing, the attendants tightly wrapped me in a large bath towel. Since the bathwater is not heated, I was expecting to be very cold. I wasn't. During the baths, everyone is given two opportunities to say a prayer—I said mine silently. As I was getting out of the baths, my hands and feet were very warm. Being a scientist, I suspected the warmth must have been due to the tightly wrapped towel.

As soon as I dressed, I tried to find my wife so we could continue the day's tour together. I couldn't find her, so I started back to the hotel to get a warm sweater and take my pain pills. As I got halfway there, I realized I was no longer cold. I was still very warm but continued to the hotel so I could take my pills. After a few steps, I realized my leg no longer ached at all—the first time in a long time. Before I returned to the tour, I got coffee and pondered the experiences. My leg has never ached since. And I never needed a coat for the rest of the Europe tour.

Not knowing what to conclude, I told this experience to others. Some said it was a miracle. One said, "Stop analyzing it and just accept it." Others just reached across a table and shook my hand. At a friend's home later that year, I told this experience to a young father whom I did not know and his three young children. He leaned across the table, shook my hand, and invited my wife and me to his home the next day for Christmas dinner. My judgment then and now? I really did experience a miracle at Lourdes—Lourdes is for real! Were the Virgin Mary's apparitions at Lourdes, Fatima, and Guadalupe real? It's my judgment they were. I have been to two of the sites and have experienced miracles at both. I look forward to visiting Our Lady of Guadalupe in Mexico City, the most visited Catholic pilgrimage site in the world and the world's third most-visited sacred site. I wonder what I will experience. Maybe I should ask for something for my great-grandchildren.

7. My Neck Injury

While trying to fix a terribly annoying truck suspension noise problem in the late 1970s, I had one of my sons monitor the suspension system while I jumped up and down inside our recreation vehicle. Unfortunately, I hit the back of my head on the ceiling, hurting my neck. I couldn't put up soccer nets or get my hair washed (I had to use both hands to lift my head above the sink rim) without suffering severe neck pain. I got so used to the pain I stopped mentioning the problem to doctors even when they did a full-skull MRI for a constant sinus headache problem. I lived with the neck pain and inability to move my head in certain circumstances for over twenty-five years.

Decades later, during a church service, our pastor stopped his sermon and said, "I want to pause and just tell you, if you need help with something or just have a question, ask God." That night, before I went to sleep, I asked God to fix my neck. The next morning as I was going about my usual routine, I suddenly realized I did not have any neck pain, regardless of my head's position. It has been over a decade since, and I have not experienced any discomfort doing anything!

A miracle? I am not the only one who thinks so. While on a church tour, our pastor asked us if anyone on the bus wanted to lead in singing a song, tell an interesting story, or share a miracle. I later told him about my neck experience. Later during the trip, he came to the back of the bus and asked if I wanted to share my neck experience. I declined because of a similar experience at Lourdes, France. Though different in nature, I couldn't tell one experience without including the other. I did not know if the pastor had heard about the Lourdes experience. I declined the invitation. Telling both experiences seemed self-aggrandizing—I feared what others might think.

Later during the bus trip, we visited the convent where St. Bernadette of Lourdes lived out her short life. In the museum containing her last belongings and writings, I noticed a two-inch-by-one-inch handwritten note asking why more people don't write about sin. In retrospect, we all have different experiences and should be more willing to communicate those experiences to others. There will always be some people who find spiritual experiences just stories that are not logical, rational, or prudent to believe. That's the whole point. Once one has such experiences, it is not logical, rational, or prudent to not be aware of the ultimate reality—God, Satan, the saints, and the deceased are real and interact with us. I wish I was more aware when I was younger and less concerned about what others might think. We should share our experiences with others without regard as to what they might think. Maybe they, too, will become aware of the ultimate reality. Maybe they, too, will be invited to a complete stranger's family Christmas dinner.

8. Funerals

I first met John during an interview for a principal system engineering position at a university research laboratory. He was the laboratory deputy director. In his early sixties, John was a caring, gentle man, well educated, quiet, and sensitive toward others. A little over a year after I started working at the lab, John suddenly passed away.

His funeral was well attended at a local church, a church he helped build. The rain was very heavy. It was one of the darkest and rainiest Northwest days I had ever seen. I don't remember any sun breaks. As I listened to his daughter and several friends address John's life and their relationship, I realized John was indeed a special person. Out of a sense of friendship (agape love, if you will), I thought, *If I could, I would do something special, like light up John's coffin.* I knew such a thing was impossible in the middle of such a service. Every light was turned on that could be turned on. And the weather was so bad. (Throughout this book I use the term "agape love" as reflective of God's unconditional affectionate love. C. S. Lewis describes *agape* as the highest level of love known to humanity: a selfless love passionately committed to the well-being of others (p. 70 in *The Four Loves*.)

Almost instantly, the priest stopped his sermon and said, "I don't know if you have noticed, but John's coffin is lit up!" And then the priest said something about how appropriate or special it was. Being short and sitting so far back, I couldn't see the coffin over the tall, young men in front of me. Apparently, the coffin was the only thing in the altar area that was lit up. How? By a brief burst of the sun's rays coming through a skylight I hadn't noticed? A divine spiritual event?

Although this wasn't the first or the last time I realized I could will (or even just wish) for something and have it actually happen, it was one of the most exhilarating. Are other people aware and capable of such experiences? Why hadn't I heard of others' experiences like this? It is my judgment that two such disparate events happening within a second, strictly by coincidence, is impossible. It is my judgment God concurred with my feelings of agape love for John and lit up his coffin.

As I look back on this experience after many years, I think I know why it happened. While not a student of the Bible, I recently found the following statements:

> *Whoever abides in love, abides in God and God abides in that person. (1 John 4:16)*
> *If you abide in me, and my words abide in you, ask for whatever you wish, and it will be done for you. (John 15:4–17, English Standard Version of the Holy Bible, 2001, Crossway Bibles)*

Over a decade later, I attended a funeral mass for a lady I did not know. Her two adult children were there. Of course the preceding experience came to mind. I didn't see how any such event was possible in the present church. And I couldn't justify willing such an event because I didn't know her. But I asked God anyway to do something similar. When the pastor was done with his eulogy, he asked the deceased lady's two children if they had anything to add. Even though neither of the children had planned on saying anything, as each started to speak, the power in the church had a glitch, once for each child. The outage was very short—hardly noticeable. Wow. Had He answered my request? And picked the right moment to do it? I wondered what caused the problem—maybe something localized to the church. When we returned home later that afternoon, I had to reset all our home's electric clocks—apparently the Boss wanted me to know He was responsible! The outage was widespread.

9. A Friend's Bout with Cancer

A coworker and I ran four miles a day two to three times a week at a local track. He was younger and in much better condition than I was. During one of our runs, I asked him about his cholesterol. Based on a medical article I had read, his cholesterol was way too low. He was at high risk for cancer—something I regret not discussing with him.

Later that year, he was taken to a large local hospital and told he had a rare form of cancer. After researching the prognosis for that type of cancer, I found such patients had only a 5 percent chance of surviving the first year. When I visited him in the hospital, he reached out to shake my hand. I reached out and shook his hand despite having had a malignant melanoma mole removed from the palm of my hand the day before. My hand had stiches and was very sore. As I was leaving, I asked God to see that my friend would be okay. My friend returned to work for a short period, applied for an early medical retirement, and sadly left for what we all thought would be a short life. I saw him again eight years later at a local store. We didn't discuss his condition. After another four years, I had a business phone conversation with his wife. When I asked how her husband was doing, she said, "He is still alive."

It's experiences like this that make me wonder, if we ask God for something, with agape love in our heart, will he act? Many other personal experiences confirm that God does answer our requests. So why the mole on my hand at that time and place? It just didn't seem like coincidence. I have since concluded it was Satan's doing. He did not want me to touch my friend. Just asking God for my friend to be okay may not have been enough. If Satan was involved, he is truly omnipresent and powerful. But maybe Satan doesn't know the future.

10. My Stepson's Attention-Deficit Disorder (ADD)

When I first noticed my stepson might be hyperactive, I sat him on my lap and we played a game. I held his hands to see if he could keep his feet from moving. He could not. Then I held his feet to see if he could keep from moving his hands. He could not. I realized he probably had ADD. His mother and I enrolled him in a Lutheran school first-grade class with a teacher who was educated and experienced in teaching children with ADD. The next year we enrolled him in a public school. Midway through the year, I received a call from my stepson's principal. They could not find him. She was required by school district policy to call the police. The principal called me at work and asked me to come to the school. His mother could not be reached. I was in the middle of a design division project review meeting, which I postponed, and went immediately to the school. After being briefed on the situation, I walked to my stepson's classroom to try to retrace his steps. As I walked through the library, a little boy came running out from somewhere in the library and grabbed on to my leg and would not let go. It was my stepson. As we drove home, he asked, "Are you angry with me?" I said, "No, we will just spend a lazy day together."

Shortly after this experience, I ended up taking my stepson to the local university's children's hospital to have the situation analyzed by a world expert. During the first session with the university psychologist, I asked my stepson, "What does Daddy Randy [me] do to get your attention?" My stepson responded, "You give me a love tap." And I said, "How do I feel about that?" He responded, "You hate doing that." I asked, "Why do I hate that?" He responded, "Because you love me so much." The psychiatrist didn't comment. It seemed he didn't quite know how to respond.

After a few sessions, the doctor's diagnosis was attention-deficit hyperactivity disorder (ADHD). The doctor prescribed a drug (state-of-the-art at the time) that would help alleviate the effects of the disorder. I arranged a school telephone conversation with the doctor, my stepson's principal, and the school district's psychologist to help educate everyone on how to handle an ADHD child. My stepson did fine through the rest of his grade-school classes. Neither of his parents attended any of the university medical center or school meetings. Several years after his mother and I divorced, I ran into my stepson's family members at a local restaurant and asked how he was doing. I believe he was in high school at the time. They said he was doing fine. It was my stepdaughter who was having problems. It's my judgment that my love for my stepson, with a helping hand from God, ensured my stepson was okay. To this day, I love the memories of every moment I spent with my stepchildren. It's my judgment that when we seek His direct intervention and do everything we can, a positive result can be considered a miracle. What prompts Him to act? He shares our love.

III

Direct Interventions

When you hear a voice from the ultimate reality, you have just experienced a direct intervention.

11. My Son's Hip Problem

Many years ago, when my oldest son was still in his early teens, he developed a serious limp when he walked. Everything looked normal with both legs. They were the same length, and it didn't hurt when he put his weight on either leg. Yet when he walked, he limped. He could not play soccer, which he dearly loved. While I was working, his mother took him to first one local doctor and then another. This process took several days. The use of strong prescription analgesics made no difference in his limp. Finally, an orthopedic surgeon did full body x-rays using the newest technology called computed tomography (CT). When I came home from work the day my son's CT scans had been analyzed, my wife told me the consensus of the doctors was our son may have a tumor at the base of his spine. The rapid onset of symptoms indicated the possibility of a cancerous tumor. The local doctors recommended we take our son to the major regional university hospital. The local doctors provided copies of the CT x-rays and made the referral to the university children's hospital.

I was beside myself. As any parent who has faced such an ordeal can attest, I felt an overwhelming sense of despair. While my wife attended to my son in his bedroom, I went into the kitchen and sat down at the dining table with my head in my hands. I am not sure who I thought I was talking to in my mind, but I thought, *I can't live with this! I can't lose my son!* Suddenly, I heard the thought, **He is okay.** It wasn't a feeling or a wishful thought. The Voice, as I now call it, was like someone had spoken to me, but I did not hear it through my ears. My despair immediately started to fade—I believed the Voice! I am not sure why. This was the first time I heard the Voice, but it would not be the last.

Two days later, we took my son to the university hospital. As we waited in the lobby to be called to an examination room, a little girl—I think she said she was six—sat down beside me. She was very talkative and wanted to know why we were there. I told her about our son's condition. She told me about her cancer and how the chemotherapy had caused her to lose all her hair. When my name was called, I stood up and said goodbye and wished her well. She did the same. If I had known then what I know now, I would have asked the Boss to intervene on her behalf.

We were led to a large examining room with a window overlooking the hospital grounds. As instructed by a nurse, my wife and I helped our son change into a hospital garment and climb on to the examining table. Shortly thereafter, a team of doctors and students came into the room. Following introductions, the doctor in charge, a department head, and another senior doctor from a different department examined our son by moving his legs around and asking him questions about the pain. Following the brief exam and a question-and-answer session with the students, the team left the room to review the CT scans.

While we were waiting for the doctors to return, I went over to the window and gazed out at the cherry trees in full bloom. My thoughts drifted to formulating our summer plans. I turned to my wife and said, "When do you think we should go camping?" In an angry voice, she said, "How can you think of something like that at a time like this?" I had not told her about the Voice. Even though I wasn't really worried about my son, I pondered the voice experience.

What did "he is okay" mean? Would he still need surgery? My sense was to keep the experience to myself.

When the two senior doctors opened the examining room door, they were laughing about something—we never knew what. Embarrassed, the lead doctor apologized. They told us they did not believe the image shown on the CT scans was a tumor. It was their judgment that our son had two problems—a dry hyperextended hip from playing soccer, and scoliosis or curvature of the spine. They summarized by recommending he stay off his feet for a week. As he left the room, the lead doctor turned back and said, "He is okay," the exact same words as the Voice!

Pondering this experience, I wondered, Did I hear an angel's voice? God's? Did God opt to allay my despair? As a relatively young scientist, I was not prepared for what might have been such an overt spiritual experience. I never told anyone about the Voice until a couple of decades later—who would believe it? I was not sure I believed it until I had many more such experiences.

12. A Promotion, a Skiing Trip, and a Divorce

A little background is in order here. I understand most intimate partnerships change over time; we either accept (which may mean forgiving), adjust, or leave. Communication is certainly important and must be a first step. But sometimes baring our feelings is not enough. When we face loss of a long-term affectionate, intimate relationship through separation or divorce, most of us are filled with great despair and emptiness. To complicate matters, who we are partially depends on past psychological traumas, genetics, physical well-being, the culture we live in, and other factors. We all have different personality profiles that change with, among other things, age, life experiences, and home and work environments. Who we are is significantly affected by our society's spirituality, ethics, morality, and whatever we need to do to survive emotionally and physically. I don't think the effects of these psychological and cultural issues can be understated during separations. But they are not the focus of this book. (I can't emphasize enough the urgency to seek professional help if one cannot work through situations of great despair on his or her own.) Literature is full of many references on these subjects. I found some of them useful. None, however, prepared me for the life-changing spiritual experiences I was about to encounter.

Decades ago my first marriage was in trouble and had been for several years. My wife was in love with someone else. I was numb, indifferent to life. I was merely going through the motions of living. My children had grown up and left. I was alone. When my wife was home, she was indifferent and preoccupied. One year when we went on vacation, I tried to stop at a few visitors' spots to take pictures and just enjoy the rugged beautiful Northwest Cascades. My wife would have none of it; she was in a hurry to get home.

At about the same time, I added another source of anxiety to my life. I had applied for a new position as head of a design engineering division. There were over sixty applicants. I wasn't hopeful.

Later that year, we went cross-country skiing with my wife's employer and his wife. I knew something was wrong with my marriage, but I did not know my wife was having an affair with her boss. While my wife skied with him, his wife followed way back. I lagged far behind. It was the first time I had gone cross-country skiing, and we were on an intermediate run. We stayed in a condominium for three nights, skiing two full days. I was frustrated and exhausted. On the third day, we left early so we could stop and ski at a downhill ski resort—that I could do.

As I drove while the other three talked, I suddenly felt this intense feeling of joy. The word *joy* doesn't really do the sensation justice. I felt it more in the center of my chest than anywhere else. I didn't know what to make of it. Somehow, I sensed I had received the work promotion I had applied for months earlier. I thanked God for telling me. Since the feeling continued, I told (when I say this, I mean I thought) Him, *I don't need to feel the sensation anymore—it's kind of scary."* I regret thinking that now. I should have relished the sensation longer. It's not often one directly feels God's love or joy. It had never happened to me before. I never hinted or said a word to the others in the car. Immediately after the sensation left, I told God,

Since you're here, I don't know if you know or care, but I am lonely. He responded later that day.

When we got to the downhill ski area, my wife and her boss went to more advanced slopes while his wife skied the beginners' slope. Not wanting to ski alone, I stayed with his wife. We talked almost constantly as we rode the chairlifts and skied. For the first time in years, I didn't feel alone.

A year passed with no changes in my marriage. One day, I wasn't feeling well and made a doctor's appointment. He got me right in and gave me a complete physical, including blood tests. The morning I went in to get the test results I was almost too sick to drive. But I went. The doctor told me my neutrophil white blood cell count was virtually zero and my eosinophil count was high, indicating a serious infection, probably viral. He took additional blood tests, including an HIV test, and put me on an antibiotic one thousand times stronger than the strongest tetracycline. I was panic-stricken.

Since I was too sick to go to work, I went home. As soon as I got home, I turned on the stereo, made myself a bourbon drink, went out on the patio, and sat down on the cold concrete with my legs folded under me. It was certainly one of my greatest moments of despair. I told the Boss my sense of things was that He wanted me to stay in my marriage, which I found equally disparaging in addition to being seriously ill. Why else would He allow me to be so sick with potential consequences so serious? So I told Him I surrendered to his will and would stay in my marriage. Immediately I heard the Voice for the second time in my life say, *I am not asking you to stay, I am asking you to live.* This time, the voice was loud, authoritative, and direct.

Believe me, it is scary to hear directly from God the Father—it is a life-changing experience. No doubt about it this time, I had heard directly from the great "I am who I am." A few days later I was feeling fine—no fever, no chills. During my next visit, the doctor told me my second set of blood tests all came back normal, including the differentiated white blood cell count. I often wonder if I had food poisoning. The day before I got sick, a group of fellow employees and I had eaten lunch at a buffet. By the time I got to the buffet line, it was the end of the lunch period—most of the food was gone. I took the last serving of potatoes mixed in a white cream sauce that had been sitting out for hours. That would have explained the blood test results as well as the symptoms, timing, and duration of my illness.

I still think about God's choice of words. He was *asking*. I take it by His response He was actively involved in the entire event. Does this experience mean we really do have free will with a little directional help from God? By not being sick, I had my life ahead of me. I was certainly motivated to *live*. But what did He mean specifically by "live"? It certainly wasn't to continue existing as I had been.

He was not asking me to leave my marriage either. When I asked my wife to leave her position, she slugged me in the shoulder so hard it hurt for three days. In the spirit of forgiveness, I still gave the marriage a second chance, but it failed. I filed for divorce a few years later. What is the value of fidelity in a romantic relationship? Intimacy and affection. Once it is gone you know it.

Lessons Learned

What did this experience teach me? God, the Father, is—period! His existence is not just something I believe; it is something I know. He directly interacts in our lives. He guides us to make better choices. To what purpose? In my case, it was to "feel"—that's exactly what I was not doing. Feel what? Many things, including love, satisfaction in creating (painting, writing, building, and so on), dancing, singing, listening to music, camping, fishing, and anything that brings joy, happiness, and appreciation for our beautiful lives and planet. I had not done any of those things in a long time.

But what specifically did God mean by "live"? Shortly after this experience, I was watching a movie based on a science fiction novel. At the end of the movie, seemingly unrelated to the subject, the narrator indicated that the author of the book on which the movie was based had ended the book with a definition of "live"—fall in love, write a book, and be passionate about something. Just coincidence? I think not!

There are many other implications from this experience. He will answer us directly when we are suffering great despair. Talking directly to Him requires strong belief, a high state of grace, and surrendering to His will. I will discuss additional lessons learned from this experience later, including how it has affected my ability to commune in many other ways with the great "I am who I am." Imagine the implications of this experience. He cares. What we do and how we feel matter to Him—our life has purpose and meaning to Him! Moments count. Sometimes God uses suffering and pain to enrich our lives and act as a comparative baseline for all other feelings. Maybe without suffering and pain we would get apathetic. Why doesn't He talk to us more often? If He did, maybe we would stop trying to live and obsess on the hereafter.

13. Cancer Diagnosis and the Voice

As mentioned before, the Boss and I have had words on using health issues to motivate me. Especially real ones. I lose hope. That's not a good thing. Did the Boss listen? You be the judge.

Eighteen years ago, I went to my dermatologist for a biannual checkup. He had removed basal and squamous cell carcinomas before—none of which had resulted in serious health issues. This time, he took a biopsy from my face and didn't say anything reassuring like he had done before. Two weeks later, I went back to get the results. As I left my car and started to walk to the doctor's office, I heard the Voice for the third time in my life: **Whatever happens here, you will be okay.** My first thought was *Uh-oh*. The tests were positive. But by this time I had learned when the Voice says you will be okay, everything really will be okay.

When the doctor came into the examining room, he told me the tests were positive for basal cell carcinoma. The surgery the following week took longer than a major surgery I had earlier in my life. As the doctor was about to start the surgery, he warned me I could end up with partial facial paralysis. I just shrugged—I knew I was going to be okay. Apparently, this type of carcinoma can metastasize.

Five percent of all brain cancers are caused by basal cell carcinoma. I didn't know that at the time. It wouldn't have mattered. *He* said I would be okay. And I was.

Whenever I heard the Voice on a medical issue, there has been a problem. Whenever I have not heard the Voice on medical issues, there were no problems. Remember, these interactions all started with mental communes with God—mostly one way, from me to him. As I have discussed before, His reactions can take many forms, including the Voice, or silent positive responses that just happen, including premonitions, precognitions, or sudden feelings of peace or joy. Don't wait for Him to talk or communicate with you. Sometimes when you're worried or need something, you can just ask. You can respectfully ask any question, including asking for His direct intervention. You can even ask for miracles. When you commune with the Boss, *always surrender to His will.* Ask only for things you or someone else needs. It's okay to wish for other things, but it seems disrespectful to ask for excessive opulence in any form. Such requests may distract from God's plans—a lesson I learned well while writing this book. Remember, God is about unconditional love—love of others, love of life, and love of His creation. He is not about lust, power, fame, and fortune. He just wants you to enjoy each day and help Him take care of His world. Remember, the opposite of love isn't hate. It's selfishness. Throughout my life, He has frequently made me aware of opportunities to thrive and help others survive. Unfortunately, I can't count the number of times I failed to act on those intuitive feelings.

14. My Father's Illness and the Voice

Many years ago, I had to drive eight hundred miles after work to my sister's home. My father had suffered a severe heart attack. It was a long, rainy night. When going through an intervening state, I was virtually the only car on the road and driving well over the speed limit when I suddenly had an intuitive sense to slow down. A state police car passed me doing over one hundred miles an hour. I never saw the police car again. Wondering where the intuitive sense came from, I continued on my way at a more normal speed.

The late hours, bad weather, and nearly being arrested for reckless driving paled compared to concern for my father's health. By three in the morning, I was two-thirds of the way there. It was raining extremely hard. My total attention was on the road. Suddenly, I heard the Voice for the fourth time in my life: **Whatever happens down here, it will be okay.** Had God responded to my despair? Yes. I was at peace knowing everything would be okay.

When I first saw Dad in the hospital, he was upbeat, almost chipper. He did not know the results of his treadmill tests indicated no normal change in blood pressure with treadmill speed and duration. Something was seriously wrong with him. With other family members, I stayed a short time to help my sister get him into a Veteran's Administration hospital. My father was retired and living only on social security. He had no health insurance other than his veteran benefits. We would not find out for several weeks how serious his condition really was. My father was fortunate enough to have a triple bypass, valve replacement, and a heart chamber repaired at a major university medical center by one of the two best cardiac surgical teams in the world—at no cost to him or the family. He survived many more years.

Whenever you hear the Voice of God, believe—it will be as He says. I haven't heard the voice lately in my life—I just know. Asking seems to have taken its place. When I ask, and it doesn't happen, I know it will be okay. I feel God's feelings directly now. I recognize His or Satan's interventions and interactions.

15. The Evil One

Refrigerator Magnet

One day my stepchildren and I were eating lunch at the kitchen table. I don't remember how or why the discussion of Satan's existence came up, but it did. My stepchildren were about seven and nine at the time. I explained my view on the subject and gave them a sense of why I thought Satan was real. I explained the story of how the archangel Lucifer had displeased God and how Lucifer had been moved far away from Him. For some reason, the three of us started chanting "down with Satan" or something to that effect.

Suddenly, a large magnet fell off the refrigerator door. As I got up to put it back on the door, I noticed there had been no papers or pictures under it. I also noticed it was very strong, by far the strongest magnet on the door. It had never fallen off before, and it never fell off again. After I returned to the table and sat down, I made the comment, "Guys, I think we were just in the presence of the evil one." The children didn't know what to make of the experience—they didn't take it as seriously as I did. I changed the subject to something less frightening to me. This was one of three times I experienced Satan's direct presence.

The lesson I learned and my advice to you, the reader, is don't scoff at or mock the evil one. You are better off ignoring him. Satan is powerful; after all, he is an archangel. Why does God allow Satan to interact with us? Maybe Satan's presence adds dimensionality to our free will. I have never asked Satan for anything. I have no intension of resonating with Satan's hate for any of us. Shakespeare said, "Love all, trust a few, do wrong to no one." I suspect Satan is very close to anyone who does not share Shakespeare's view.

Satan's Laugh

I had turned in my retirement paperwork weeks before I had reason to believe my second wife was having an affair. The timing couldn't have been worse. Since it was basically a buyout, the organization would not allow anyone to withdraw his or her retirement application. I had counted on my retirement pay and my wife's income to maintain our standard of living, at least until I had a new career. Well before my last day, I started looking for a new job. I had several interviews, but no job offers.

About a month after my retirement, school was out for summer break, so my stepchildren were at their fathers for two weeks. Thinking I might have to sell the house, I had been working very hard to fix it up. One day when the house was very quiet, I lay down for a late afternoon nap. I fell into a deep sleep. After at least an hour, I was startled awake by a *very loud, gruff laugh.* It sounded like it came from someone leaning over my bed. I checked all the closets and the rest of the house, upstairs and down. Everything was still locked. I don't know why, but I made note of the date and time.

For three weeks, I had noticed my wife was coming home late from work almost every night and leaving for work very early. With the kids gone, I thought she was just catching up on her work assignments so she could be home when the children returned. Still, she seemed distant and disinterested in remodeling the house.

The night before the Fourth of July, my wife went to bed early. I stayed up, watched a movie, and then went out onto the patio with a drink to look at the night sky. I had a sense something was wrong with our relationship. So shortly after eleven o'clock, I asked God and whatever angels may be to *let me know what is really in my wife's heart.* Suddenly, I was compelled to reconcile and balance our checkbooks. After all, I wasn't tired. So I looked for my wife's purse. When I opened it, I saw several sheets of what turned out to be her diary. I read a few pages. I had the answer to my request in my hands less than forty-five minutes after I asked.

I took the diary to a local twenty-four-hour supermarket and made a copy. By the time I got back home, it was almost two in the morning. I put the diary back in her purse. Then I read my copy. I realized the day and time I had heard the evil, scary laugh were the same day and time she had asked her lover to leave his wife and run off with her. Wow. As I pondered my situation, I had this *urge* to check her van. As I entered the driver's side, I saw her gym bag sitting between the seats. Without turning on the inside light, I searched the bag with my hands. I found three floppy disks.

As I loaded each disk on my computer, I glanced at the contents. The disks contained the last three months' emails between my wife and her lovers—yep, there was more than one. Wow again! I returned the disks to her gym bag and went back to my computer and read the emails. I had all the details. Imagine asking the Boss to know what was in someone's heart and finding out in less than forty-five minutes. I am glad I found out. But as the old saying goes, be careful what you ask for; you just might get it. If you don't want to know, don't ask.

The separation we had two months later was interesting. Together we found her an apartment but put off signing the rental agreement. One morning, while she was at work and the kids were with their father, I pondered whether I should go through with the divorce. I knew I couldn't afford to keep my house with just my retirement income. I had previously applied and interviewed for two jobs. After thinking about it, I decided to go through with the divorce, whether I lost the house or not. Within a minute after making that decision, I received a call from one of the two companies with a job offer. I accepted. A few minutes later, the second organization called with a job offer. Since I had already accepted a position with the first company, I put off considering the second job offer. Was God helping me decide? I had a choice to make. Keep the house and try to make the marriage work or start a new life and career. God's response to my asking was virtually instantaneous. He is always with us. But he lets us decide our fate.

Satan was literally involved with these events. One might say he got the last laugh. Not for me, but my ex-wife and two precious stepchildren? I asked God they all be okay.

The Bad Dream

My third direct experience with the evil one was a little subtler than the previous two. My present wife and I had found a charming little house in the Northwest woods—it was like something out of Tolkien's *Lord of the Rings*. The woods were full of raccoons, possums, and many types of birds. God knew what else. The problem? It was at least three hours from work one way. It was a gamble I decided to take.

One night before I went to bed, I told God I wanted the house. And I told Him I didn't want Him to keep us from getting it. I did not know He would move so far away from me when I said what I said the way I said it. But He did. I was on my own and didn't know it! (I was forced to sell the house in the woods a year later. The five-hour plus commute was just too long.) As we went to bed, I had no sense of what was about to happen. That night my dream was horrible. I woke up around two in the morning in a sweat. I had a bad dream. I can't describe in words what it felt like to be so far away from God's grace and love. I assure you if you ask God to leave, He will. I also assure you the evil one steps right in. Don't do it. Grace, once lost, is hard to earn back.

In summary, the evil one exists in the shadows of all our lives, moving stealthily beside us. It is part of the plan. It is part of the cost of free will, the ability to choose between different choices unimpeded. Once you have experienced and know the difference, one cannot stand being away from God's agape love.

What are Satan's distractions? Carnality, apathy, anxiety, gluttony, exaggerated self-esteem, hate, selfishness, materialism, and many others. In other words, the total opposite of agape love. Don't ever underestimate the power of Satan. He will never stop attempting to penetrate all aspects of your life. He knows and will use all your psychological quirks and fears against you. Examples of our psychological weaknesses may include fear of failure, fear of success, low self-esteem, unconscious guilt feelings, and many others—know them and be ready. Later in this book you will read about acquaintance examples of how some psychological problems are caused by parental neglect and indifference. I am sure all of us, whether we are aware or not, have and will continue to experience battles with Satan.

16. God's Intervention with Two Homes

An Early Home

Early one spring Sunday morning several decades ago, my first wife, sons, and I set out to attend church in a quaint nearby town. After church, we had breakfast and walked through the small downtown stores. Later, we drove through the nearby countryside, admiring the large single-story, country-style homes, each positioned in the center of an acre-plus lot. Large oak and evergreen trees provided shade from the warm afternoon sun. I remember wishing that just once in my life I could live in such a house. I wasn't asking God. I didn't know about the power of asking at that point in my life. I wasn't praying either. I was just wishing.

Six months later I had a new job in the Northwest and a new home in the woods on three-quarters of an acre. Our house was beautiful, everything I could have asked for—flowering dogwood trees, cathedral ceilings, large windows with beautiful views and a transparent, olive-green mahogany exterior. I enjoyed every minute of the twenty years I lived there. Thank you, God. Had He listened to my wish? It's my judgment that sometimes we get what we wish for.

There have been times in my professional career when I have sensed God's hand at work. There seems to be a resonance between our desires, needs, and God's intervention in our lives. Sometimes now I ask for His intervention. Sometimes not—it just happens. Some aspects of life seem planned. Others seem random. All seem to involve elements of choice, either mine or someone else's. Life is a grand experience. William Ernest Henley was right when said in his poem *Invictus*, "I am the master of my fate, I am the captain of my soul."

Another Home

Much later in life when I was looking for a home in a new development closer to my current employer, I found a model I really liked still under construction. It had high ceilings in the great room and two of its three bedrooms. It was very well built with six-inch walls and a large lot. The lot backed up to an all-season salmon creek with deer, raccoons, coyotes, eagles, squirrels, bobcats, and (I hoped) no bear. I decided I couldn't afford the house, so I put an offer on another model. Sometime during the next few days, I felt disappointed in the model home. I always wanted to live in a house with high ceilings. When I went to sign the final offer papers, the realtor said the model home was already sold but offered us the house I really wanted. I thanked God for his intervention. Fifteen years later, my present wife and I still live in the house. I hope this is the house we live in in heaven.

Sometimes God's interventions are miraculous. I never questioned whether I could afford the new house in retirement. When God clearly gives you something, as he did with our home, appreciate it. Don't casually give it up. You may not get a third chance.

IV

Divine Interactions

*When you experience events
that appear to be just coincidence, think again.*

17. Fatima, Portugal

For years I wondered how Christian societies could justify two issues. The first was why would truly evil people (those who inflict great harm on others) be completely forgiven in the next life without sincerely repenting in this life and changing their ways. My guess is truly evil people are not likely to repent. The second issue was how the high cost of Europe's great cathedrals could be justified in a time when most people were illiterate and barely surviving day to day. The first question was answered at Lourdes (see Malachi later in this section) and shortly after returning home from our Europe tour.

Prior to the trip, I noticed I had a blood blister on my lip, so I bought a shaving stick that would stop any bleeding if I had a problem. Unfortunately, or fortunately, depending on how you look at it, I inadvertently left the stick at home. After lunch on the first day at Fatima, we all went back to our rooms. I noticed my lip blister was bleeding profusely, so I could not attend the afternoon tour of the new large modern church. That afternoon, I finally found a small drugstore that had what I needed and rejoined the tour.

To walk into Europe's older cathedrals, especially in Paris and Rome, must have been a truly magnificent experience for all of

Europe's population. The stories in the cathedrals' artwork and glass windows depict scenes straight out of the holy book. To this day, all visitors can see and feel a bit of heaven. As to the cost? Building of the cathedrals provided jobs for the working class, which helped redistribute wealth while providing a sense of peace and security.

While watching the video of the tour, I realized I had missed seeing the inside of the new modern Fatima church. It just didn't have the feel and warmth of the older churches. Did this experience at Fatima answer my question about why the older churches meant so much to their populations, thereby justifying their construction? I believe the answer is yes. It's my judgment that my minor health problem was not a coincidence.

18. The Wheat and Weeds Parable

One warm summer afternoon we had family and friends over for a barbecue. Midway through, we were sharing stories that, to each of us, were potentially spiritual in nature. When I started talking about one of my experiences, a friend of one of the people sitting around the table kept whispering in her neighbor's ear and laughing. My immediate response was one of anger. She was new to these types of discussions, but making jokes about sharing our experiences was way out of line. I stopped talking. So did everyone else. For that night and most of the next day, I wasn't sure I wanted to continue this book. Overnight, I pondered how to deal with similar experiences should the book ever be published. The experiences of many saints, apostles, and disciples were certainly far more horrific. Yet they continued with their missions. Relatively speaking, my experience was trivial.

Though I was depressed, the next day I felt compelled to attend church. The gospel was focused on the wheat and weeds parable. Excerpts are listed below.

> *The Kingdom of Heaven is like a farmer who planted good seed in his field. But that night as the workers slept, his enemy came and planted weeds*

among the wheat, then slipped away. When the crop began to grow and produce grain, the weeds also grew.

The farmer's workers went to him and said, "Sir, the field where you planted that good seed is full of weeds! Where did they come from?"

"An enemy has done this!" the farmer exclaimed.

"Should we pull out the weeds?" they asked.

"No," he replied, "you'll uproot the wheat if you do. Let both grow together until the harvest. Then I will tell the harvesters to sort out the weeds, **tie them into bundles, and burn them,** *and to put the wheat in the barn."*

I remember thinking after church, *Thank you, God, for telling me why you allow certain people to be, at best, impolite.* It is my judgment that God couldn't allow free will without allowing people to be arrogant, self-focused, and just plain rude. I wondered if this was true for all mean and evil actions.

Many months later, I met a lady outside a local store. I was admiring her Bernese mountain dog. Her husband was in Afghanistan. Somehow our conversation drifted to spirituality. In her circumstances, I understood why she said Satan ruled this world. Even though it was a subject I knew well, I did not comment. I regret not telling her to express her regret directly to God. Feeling her despair is one of the reasons I wanted to finish writing this book as quickly as possible. A member of another church also told me Satan rules this world. I am not aware of any statement in any of the holy books that Satan rules the world. That certainly is not my experience. God rules this world. Free will requires the option of evil. Selfish choices create evil. If one wishes for power, fame, or fortune, they have just experienced a selfish thought whispered to them by Satan—a direct interaction if you will.

19. Malachi

Just prior to our church tour of Europe, I questioned whether God would forgive all evildoers. Prior to our trip, I asked my little five-year-old godson if he knew who the evildoers were. He answered, "Those who hurt good people." How perfect.

I was taught that if an evildoer confesses his or her sins, he or she will be forgiven. In my opinion, some sins are so great—How could they be forgiven? Without getting into a discussion on repentance, the question haunted me just prior to our trip. At Lourdes, France, I was assigned as a group leader to coordinate "server" participation in the daily church service. Since the service was unexpectedly scheduled half a day early, I did not have my group prepared. I arranged all functions, including assigning the first reading to myself. I did not have my reading glasses and did not have a chance to read anything ahead of time. Careless? Yes. Divine intervention? In retrospect, it was. As I started to read the first reading, I realized I could hardly see the book, so I moved the book closer then farther away, so I could at least guess at the words. The reading was from Malachi. In summary, I got to the part where it said, "All the arrogant and evildoers will be stubble, and the day that is coming will set them on fire. Not a root or a branch will be left of them… They will be ashes…" says the Lord Almighty. When I read that last part, my voice increased in volume. I realized my question had been answered. Evildoers will surely suffer the loss of eternal life if they have not sincerely repented and changed their hearts.

Shortly after we returned home from the trip, on our way to a church service, I told my wife, "I have that feeling again of anger toward evildoers." That day's gospel was from Malachi. Coincidence? I think not. God reinforced his previous answer concerning evildoers. There is an afterlife and accountability. Don't be an unrepentant evildoer! God's ethos (character/ethic) is one of love. Satan's is one of selfishness and jealousy.

20. Interactions with My Deceased Stepfather and Mother

My Stepfather's Funeral

My stepfather was born in Canada. He became a citizen of the United States of America in the early 1940s when he joined the US Army. Monteith rose to the rank of master sergeant during World War II, serving in Europe. I remember listening to his many fascinating war and postwar stories. One was most interesting. He swears he saw Adolf Hitler, after he was supposedly dead, in the window of a small mountain village building. When his platoon searched the building, they found no one. I believed my stepfather—if there was one face he knew well, it was Adolf Hitler's.

Monteith turned down a final assignment in Germany in the 1960s and retired. As he explained, he had a sense he was supposed to return to the Monterey Peninsula where he met my mother. They married and, together, raised my two sisters. After my sisters married, my mother and Monteith moved near me in the Northwest. We spent many Friday nights and most holidays together. In his early seventies, Monteith had a heart attack and desired to return to California. Within a year, he developed pancreatic cancer and passed away.

I drove eight hundred miles the day before the funeral and stayed with my brother. My two sisters stayed with our mother to comfort her. My brother and I stayed up most of the night, sharing a bottle of whisky.

At the request of my mother, I was awakened after only two hours of sleep, still reeling from the long drive and the alcohol. I could barely shower and dress for the funeral. I remember taking several analgesics for my headache and eating breakfast with several cups of coffee. I was in bad shape and embarrassed when I met my mother at the Episcopal Church. I sat beside her during the service. After my brother and both sisters gave a reading, my mother leaned over and asked if I was going to say something. I said, "No, I am not up to it." I was nauseous, tired, and my head pounded. And unlike my siblings, I had not prepared anything to say or read. I felt bad I didn't get up and say anything. So I took a few moments to reflect on the good times Monteith and I had together, how much he had meant to the family, and particularly the agape love I had for him—something I had not taken the time to feel very often. Almost instantly, I felt warm—all my discomfort left me. The headache and other discomforts were gone for several minutes. Then my discomfort returned. To this day, I am convinced Monteith gave me a hug.

This was my first experience with a deceased family member, but not the last.

My Mother's Funeral Service and Her Voice

When my mother passed away, I traveled by air to attend her burial service with my brother and sisters. It was a hard trip, five days before Christmas. I had pneumonia, two broken toes, and two work reports due at work by the first of the year. And I was facing a work layoff. But going to my mother's funeral was something I needed to do. I hadn't seen my brother and sisters for several years and wanted to be with them in our time of sorrow. I stayed with my brother.

The morning of the graveside service, my brother and I drove near the neighborhood where my mother had lived for many years. Interestingly, the main road was blocked by a large tractor, requiring we take an alternate route. Driving through the nearby housing development, we drove right past our mother's former residence. I remember commenting to my brother, "Do you think driving by Mother's old house was coincidence?" He didn't comment. I still think it was very strange. Maybe Mother wanted us to remember the good times we shared with her at her home.

Three years later, my wife and I drove down from the Seattle area to visit my brother and younger sister in California. On our way, we stopped to visit one of my wife's cousins in Sacramento. The day we left Sacramento, I didn't ask for directions to the new interstate highway. Since I had lived in California a good part of my life, I knew the roads well. I turned onto the first freeway I saw. I did not see any highway signs. After we had traveled a few miles, I realized we were on the old freeway. I turned off at the first major exit, trying to find a direct route to cut over to the newer interstate, which would take us directly to my brother's house. The road we took dead-ended. So we went back to the old highway and drove until we saw signs to the new interstate. As we took the cutoff, I realized we were in the small town where my mother had lived. Since my wife had never been there, I showed her my mother's favorite restaurants, housing development, and stores. The whole experience seemed surreal. Again, I think my mother wanted me to remember and my wife to see where she had lived. I believe the experience was not a coincidence.

More than a decade after my mother passed away, I was losing sleep worrying about how my precious wife and children would fare when I passed away. I was awakened by my mother's voice saying, "It will be okay, Randy." Randy was her nickname for me—I hadn't heard it in many years. In addition to my leg miracle at Lourdes, do you suppose my mother's voice answered *both* prayers I asked in the Lourdes baths? My first prayer was "I ask my wife be okay when I am gone." My second prayer was "I ask that my parents go to heaven." My conclusion? My mother is in heaven and my wife will be okay when I am gone. Does this experience suggest our future is a foregone reality? Is it fixed? Is there only one future? Maybe from a given point in our lives some outcomes are fixed.

What are the implications of the above experiences? When we die, we still exist and can commune subtly or directly with the living. Life after death is a reality. We need not worry about death. I still have many "awareness" questions about life, but the reality of a hereafter is no longer one of them. This happened at a time in my life when I knew God existed. After these experiences, I know, in some sense, we exist in the hereafter as more than just one of God's memories.

21. Precious Moments with Children

A Mall Trip

One rainy day, while my wife was working, I took my two stepchildren to the mall just to get out of the house. While we were walking along the concourse, my stepdaughter stopped in front of a knickknack store full of strange new-age dragon statues and other weird stuff. I wasn't really interested in going in, but I did. As the three of us walked through the store, my stepdaughter held my hand and forced me to stop, look, smell, and feel every little furry thing in the store. We even stopped to listen to mystical music CDs. As we walked out of the store, I realized I had just experienced seeing the world through the eyes of a child—how grand.

Later that same morning after we returned home, my stepdaughter wanted to watch animal shows with me—something we did almost every week. After a while, I lay down on the couch and started to drift off. Pretty soon, both my stepchildren climbed up and fell asleep on top of me. It was a little early for naps, but I lay there for almost an hour while they slept. If I had been twenty years younger, I would have pushed them off the minute I got too warm. But I realized the preciousness of the moment. I didn't move a muscle.

Though children can be great responsibilities, I suspect every moment we spend with them, at any age, lasts forever. Children add unconditional love, meaning, and purpose to our lives. They truly are a blessing from God.

My Stepson and the Little Girl

One day when I was driving my young stepson and stepdaughter to school, my stepson said, "There is this little girl that keeps bothering me at school, even when I am with my friends." I responded by saying, "Really? I know someone who loves her very much." He responded, "You do? Who?" I pointed to the sky with an upturned thumb. He responded, "Does that mean I have to love her too?" His sister, who was in the back seat, leaned forward to hear my answer. I responded, "Not necessarily in the same way, but it means you better damned well respect the fact that He loves her!" Two weeks later after a school Christmas play, my stepson's friends were encouraging him to follow them to the playground. At about the same time, the little girl came over and was talking with him. My stepson told his friends he would join them in a few minutes and continued talking with the little girl. I was very proud of him. He respected the little girl. Actions like my stepson's help others develop a sense of self-esteem and experience agape love. He had learned that *whatever bad or good you do to another, you do to God!*

Coffee Shop Experiences

One day while I was waiting for my coffee, a young couple with a very young boy entered, placed their order, and were waiting several yards from me. The little boy and I made eye contact. Suddenly, he set out as best as he could on a full run toward me with outreached hands. His father caught him by the collar just before the little guy reached me. The father apologized and said his son had never done anything like that before. This wasn't the first or last time I experienced a direct soul-to-soul interaction between myself and a child.

Two weeks later at the same coffee shop, an eleven-year-old boy, almost as tall as me, tapped me on the shoulder. I turned around, and we both just stared at each other without saying a word. My sense is we were communicating in a nonverbal "feeling" way. His mother intervened and apologized, saying her son thought I was his grandmother. It's true we both had orange tops, but his grandmother was in between us. He had to reach around her.

It seems to me these kinds of experiences are like two souls communicating in a manner I can't explain. It is my judgment that children are far more aware than most of us adults. Relish those moments. In some way, children are more sensitive to the ultimate reality than adults. Maybe they simply have a new, unfiltered way of sharing agape love. Unlike adults, they can believe the unbelievable and act accordingly.

Church Summer Picnic

During a recent summer picnic, we all gathered outside on blankets to eat our food. My wife and I brought a blanket and laid it on the ground. Two other families joined us. One family had a young blond son. While we were all talking, the little blond son came over and laid his head on my shoulder. We shared an ephemeral moment that I will never forget. Young children seem to have an innate ability to express agape love, even to a stranger. God is with all children. Those who harm a child hamper their own ability to ever become aware of the ultimate reality and close to God. And maybe, their very existence in the next life.

My Children's Operations

One of my sons and my stepdaughter both had major surgeries on the same day in two different hospitals in one of our major cities. The experience was traumatic for them, my wife, and me. One had cancer and the other major surgery to correct internal injuries probably caused by an automobile accident. Both had follow-up procedures, and one is still under medical care. During our hospital stay, observations and conversations with young children, some patients themselves, made me doubly aware of how fragile life is. I could not help asking God to take care of each child, not just ours. My children are okay for the moment, and I trust God will take care of all the other precious children. Maybe that's why God put us through the ordeal, knowing I would ask Him for all the children to be okay. Of course, I will never know about the others. But God knows. Maybe my request freed God to act in a manner He couldn't otherwise have done. I am glad I had the opportunity.

A Day with My Great-Grandchildren, Sons, and Granddaughter

I spent last Father's Day being entertained by my three great-grandchildren (six, four, and two), my granddaughter, and my two sons. We had a great time. My oldest son barbecued steak and salmon, which went well with our Port wine. My three great-grandchildren played with their new toys, ran through sprinklers, and held tightly on to my wife's leg when they wanted something to eat or drink. My granddaughter briefed us on her successful dog-breeding business. She is managing it very professionally. I am very proud of her. My time spent with my sons and daughter-in-law was very enjoyable. I wish we could all get together more often. But everybody is so busy and working so hard.

My three little great-grandchildren were excited about everything going on. It was joyful having little ones in the house again. I miss experiencing the sheer joy in just being alive that children instinctively express with every word and action. The whole experience reminded me of my grandmother's comment when I was young: "Enjoy your childhood—it's the best time of your life." It is my view that children are born beatified (holy). Their innocence lets them experience the world through the eyes of God. I ask God, again, to take care of every member of my family. Our love for our children, and theirs for us, is reflected in their eyes the moment they are born. That love can last for a lifetime if we unconditionally reflect it back. It's the closest to God's agape love we can directly experience. It's the reason I have, many times, asked God to protect children around the world.

Precious Moments with Our Godchildren

My wife and I spent several years helping take care of our two (who we called) our godchildren. Our godson was two months old when we started taking care of him two to three days a week. Two years later, our "goddaughter" came into our life. She was about a month old. When she tried to hold her head up to see the world, on occasion, I would put my right forefinger below her head so she could rest her chin on my finger and look around. The years my wife and I spent helping taking care of our godchildren filled our lives with great joy. When we decorated the house for holidays, they were thrilled, especially with the Christmas trees. They would study every ornament. We miss the joy they brought into our lives every day they were here. Again, don't miss a moment with children—it truly is the closest experience you will ever have to sharing and feeling God's agape love.

22. Precious Moments with Animals

Hummingbirds

One spring day as I was showering, I looked out the bathroom window and saw an incredible sight—a beautiful hummingbird thirty feet away with a brilliant metallic blue breast. As it flew away to my right, I thought, *Wow. I will never see anything like that again.* A few seconds later, it flew from my right within inches of my window, paused in the air, and turned its breast toward me for several seconds before flying away. Wow again! I think God was showing off, as well He should. A neighbor suggested it was really an angel. Either way, I thank God for sharing His beautiful creature with me. It's small moments like this that convince me "He is," cares, and wants to share His creation with us. I won't ever forget the experience. I wonder if heaven has such beautiful creatures. I hope it does.

A few years later as I sat inside my open garage enjoying the morning with my coffee, I was pondering whether to research what agnostic atheists and some academics have to say about the ultimate reality. ("Agnostic atheists are atheistic because they do not hold a belief in the existence of any deity and agnostic because they claim the existence of a deity is either unknowable in principle or currently unknown in fact" [en.wikipedia.org/wiki/Agnostic atheism

12/16/2017].) Do they give a second thought to the possibility of God, Satan, and life after death? I know their answer. The only logical, rational, prudent way to view life is through direct observation—what we can see and measure! No wonder we seem incapable of solving some of the world's and humanity's greatest problems. Couldn't we do the same with just computers? Don't feelings, experience, intuition, and empathy have any value?

When I decided to focus only on my personal experiences and their meaning to me in this book, a hummingbird flew within three feet of my face and, while hovering, looked at me first with one eye and then the other before flying away. And guess what? Seconds later, she returned and looked at me again, first with one eye and then the other, only much closer. Did God use Mother Nature to confirm my decision? I believe he did. The experience was unique and highly unlikely. Come on, a second close flyby? Have you ever had such a unique experience? I'll bet you have and, maybe, never gave it a second thought, concluding it was just coincidence.

My experiences in this book conclusively prove to me there is an ultimate reality that is always with us even when we are asleep. Examine your own past experiences and observations with an open mind. Ponder your feelings at the time. Did you sense anything? Did the nearly simultaneous occurrence of two dissimilar unrelated events seem like just coincidence? Being aware results in learning how to tell whether or not an experience is likely just a coincidence.

Cats and Dogs

I have had many pet cats in my life. The first was Caesar, a male calico cat. A vet asked if he could buy Caesar so his DNA could be studied at a local university. Apparently, only one in a thousand survive birth. Ours survived twenty years and weighed twenty-plus pounds. He would stay away for two or three nights at a time. He was constantly needing medical care to close wounds he obtained in fights with raccoons and other animals. For years he slept under my covers by my bare feet. He attacked me once from under the TV I was watching. He had one claw waving in the air. I couldn't move fast enough. His paw hit me on the side of the head. Maybe he thought I was threatening him. Maybe he just didn't recognize me. Cats see differently than we do. After the attack, I chased him down to a far corner in the house and, after closing the door behind me and putting two beds against the wall, grabbed him by the scuff of the neck and gently escorted him out of the house. He returned that night for dinner. That night, as always, he kept my feet warm.

My wife and I have had four loving cats—all feral. Ming-Ming would only come around to eat the food we put out on our deck at night so he wouldn't be seen. The only thing I ever saw was his tail disappearing off the deck. One warm day while my wife was out of the house, I accidently left the back door and screen door open and went to the farthest bedroom (my office). Ming-Ming suddenly appeared beside my desk, jumped up on the desk top, and lay down in front of me. I couldn't believe it. I started petting him and marveling at his long fur. As I was doing so, I invited God to come and see this beautiful creature He had created. Ming-Ming never left me after that. My wife took a picture of me asleep sitting up on our living room couch with Ming-Ming draped over my right shoulder, his head on my chest. He was also asleep.

I am going to spend some time on the next experience because it illustrates how little we really know about God's love for His creatures. During the same time frame, we were visited by another homeless cat we named Ling-Ling. She slept on the backyard deck in a box with a blanket—it was her home. Gigantic raccoons and possums used to come to eat from a bowl of dog food we kept on the deck— bad idea. Once I saw a big possum investigate Ling-Ling's box while she was sleeping. But the possum left her alone. During this period, Ling-Ling was pregnant twice, but I never saw any kittens. I assume wild animals ate them all. Then one afternoon, my wife and I were in the backyard when Ling-Ling stuck her head out of the box and started to meow. I went to investigate. She was in the process of delivering kittens. I helped her deliver nine kittens. We kept two and saw that the others were given to caring owners. When we moved to our new house, we brought Ming-Ming, Ling-Ling, and two of Ling-

Ling's kittens with us. Ming-Ming was driven off the property by another male cat—I hope he found a good home. Ling-Ling stayed with us, often clawing at our bedroom window screen at night asking to get in. She slept by my wife and me, often climbing on to the bed on my bare legs with her open claws. Ouch—but I always let her stay. She passed away about eight years later. We still have her two kittens, Tigger and Fluffy, who keep us company every day. Tigger sometimes comes into our bedroom at about 2:00 a.m. and just sits by the bed purring.

I remember frequently visiting Ling-Ling and her kittens in our previous home's garage. One, Tigger, used to crawl to the sound of my voice before she could open her eyes or walk. It was as though she remembered the sound of my voice and how much she would be loved. How? Einstein said we can remember the future if the entropy in the universe isn't changing (and I believe science's current view is the entropy in the universe is not changing). I don't need Einstein's view; it's obvious Tigger remembered the future sound of my voice and how much she would be loved.

Our American Eskimo dog, Angel, has been our constant companion the last fourteen years. Life just wouldn't be the same without him. He is the most loving, most sensitive companion anyone could ask for. At times, he will attempt to talk to us. And he is an excellent guard dog. Early one Easter morning (two o'clock) he started barking at the front door. When I went to investigate, I saw a large bare human footprint on the front porch. Apparently, Angel had scared away whoever it was. I believe spitz breed dogs were used by the Romans as guard dogs. I am sure Angel is related.

A few years ago, my wife had to have her heart checked at a local university. The clinic was very professional. The lead cardiologist had already analyzed the real-time EKG results before he entered the room. My wife was okay. The nurse, my wife, and I were talking about our animals as the doctor came in. Overhearing the conversation, he said, "I don't live with animals." I still feel sorry for him. He will never experience a pet's unconditional love—a love, I believe, reflective of God's love for us and all His other creations.

The Crow and the Snake

As my wife and I were about to enter our driveway one day, we noticed a crow trying to devour a rather large garden snake. After we parked, I went back to see how the crow was doing. The crow had apparently flown off with the snake in its beak. Later that day, the crow was sitting in a tree surveying the neighborhood. My wife later told me she had encountered two large snakes in our backyard and had expressed her concern to our daughter that one of us or our animals might be bitten by the snakes. My wife said, "Maybe seeing the crow with the snake means I don't have to worry about snakes." She then said to me, "Do you think that was just a coincidence?" She then answered her own question, "I don't think it was a coincidence." I agreed. Sometimes seeing such random events may serve a purpose. My wife loves to work in our backyard with our dog nearby. And now she can continue to do so. Does God assign his angels to act when we feel fearful about continuing to do something we enjoy? Since He shares my wife's joy working in the yard, you can bet He acts. Wouldn't you? If free will isn't an issue, we don't have to ask. He just acts.

23. Other Interactions

Interaction on Behalf of an Acquaintance

While attending a holiday celebration at a friend's home, I met one of my friend's family members for the first time. He was wealthy, had two homes and a thriving business. He talked mostly about how well he was doing. It was a long day. I do not know much else about him. When one of his relatives was playing drums and a guitar in the yard, the wealthy gentleman seemed annoyed. I thought the music was appropriate and entertaining. When my wife and I were leaving the driveway, I asked God (always deferring to His will) to teach the wealthy gentleman what life was all about—even if He had to "bat the gentleman upside the head with a two-by-four." Six months later at another family function, the wealthy gentleman talked for fifteen minutes about his medical problems over the last six months. He had a toe problem requiring multiple surgeries. He was allergic to everything—the antiseptics, analgesics, and other drugs used during and after the surgeries. He had to be readmitted to the hospital more than once, couldn't work full-time, and had considered suicide. I told another friend the story and said, "I hope I wasn't responsible in some way." My friend said, "You released God to act. Apparently, God agreed with you. What and how God responds is His business." The wealthy gentleman did have a completely different demeanor the second time we met.

Pastor Interactions

When our pastor announced he had been our pastor for almost as long as allowed, I was disappointed. I asked God that he be allowed to stay another tour and gave my reasons, including the sincere and emotional quality of his sermons. Sometime later, my wife came home from a church function saying our pastor had made an announcement. I said, "I know, he is staying." My wife asked, "Who told you?" I said, "No one. I asked God our pastor stay and gave Him my reasons." She knows God sometimes seems to respond to my requests in some manner. No response means He may not agree. That's okay. I ask anyway.

I once expressed concern over my progress on this book to a pastor. I told him what the book was about and said, "You know about one or two of my experiences. But the book already has many more. And I am stuck. I just don't know how to present each subject in a manner the reader will consider believable." Our pastor said, "Just tell them what it means to you," which I have done. Another time, I told the pastor my science and engineering education sometimes seemed intolerant of religious tenets. He leaned over and whispered, "Science proves the existence of God," a much different response than the comment I heard from a pastor three decades earlier when

I was in college. Being aware results in learning to tell whether or not an experience is likely just a coincidence. Coincidence may be required, to some degree, to maintain free will.

A previous pastor once interrupted his sermon announcing, "I think you should know, some people are born beatified." He certainly was. I think there are times when all of us are in a high state of grace (holy). I believe all children are born beatified, regardless of their DNA or culture. What happens to change them depends largely on their familial and societal environment.

Family Member Interactions

Over a decade ago, I realized I had no family members with whom I could share my awareness of the ultimate reality—the existence of God, Satan, and the deceased. So I asked God to help make them aware. He did so. My wife and oldest son have both responded. They are now excited about the ultimate reality and actively engage in conversations about the subject. I enjoy listening to their views and experiences. They are aware of the ultimate realities present in their lives.

My wife has shared her family experiences. Some are profound. Her mother passed away when she was only five, leaving her to care for her younger sister and baby brother. Her father worked all day. Her older brother was in school (at my wife's young age she didn't know where he went every day—she just knew he wasn't home helping her). Her experiences include hearing the voice of her mother asking her children to take care of each other. The experience was confirmed by her younger sister who still remembers their mother's voice. The rest of my wife's experiences could fill a book. Now she participates in many church functions and willingly engages in spiritual conversations with me and her friends. I think she has always been aware. Maybe my asking, in some way, freed her to express her experiences and feelings more openly.

One morning several years ago before I went to work, my wife asked me what she should do during an earthquake. I told her to get under the dining room table—it was strong enough to hold up the whole roof if it collapsed. Later that day, we experienced a level 6.8 earthquake, resulting in four hundred injuries and lasting well over thirty seconds—stronger and longer than any earthquake I ever experienced in California. The damage was over a billion dollars. Where did her precognition come from? The ultimate reality? What do you think? Before we met, my wife worked far from her home. She was so tired and the weather so bad she didn't remember driving home. At least three times, she was just suddenly at her apartment. Did she have ultimate reality guarding angels protecting her?

My oldest son has taken the possibility of an ultimate reality to heart. He and I can talk about any type of awareness experience. Once, I suggested before he attended church, ask God a question and open the Bible at random to get an answer. He's done that several times and gotten an answer. Another time, while I was trying to write this paragraph, he just happened to call (not coincidence!). He related the following story. Just as he entered church one day, he was considering whether to continue coaching and running a youth soccer program. The challenges often included dealing with parents and children with different and conflicting goals and issues. Interestingly, my son's pastor changed his sermon from his planned chapter in the Bible to the critical need to not give up an effort to help others when faced with extremely negative opposition. The pastor described how to deal with such challenges and why it is important to not give up. My son went on to redouble his volunteer efforts in the following years. His pastor gave him the exact information he needed to hear, exactly when he needed to hear it. The odds of the pastor's sermon being a random coincidence are, in my son's words, "beyond calculation." My son has told me this last experience was only one of many direct interactions he experienced during his awakening and enlightenment.

Was my awareness request for family members realized? Yes, well beyond my expectations.

Health Interactions on Behalf of a Family Friend and My Sister

A friend suffered a serious stroke and was in the hospital. It was my understanding that she couldn't speak and lost the ability to control one side of her body. Before my wife and I left home to see her, I asked God, "If she is going to survive the stroke, let her reach out and say my name." When we entered her room, I walked over to her bed. She reached out with one hand and said my name. As I held her hand, I knew she would be okay. The last time I heard she was out working in her yard when her friends drove up. When I last saw her, she still had symptoms of the stroke but was okay. Why did God allow her to have a stroke? Why didn't he heal her completely? Did He want her to change her life in some way? Maybe.

I had a similar experience with one of my sisters recently. She suffered from Alzheimer's for many years and finally had to be admitted to a specialty clinic. I don't know why, but I felt compelled to visit her. Before I left to visit, I asked God she be okay. If she was going to be okay, I asked that she recognize me. Of course I would have liked to ask she be cured, but that might not be God's will. She has lived a hard life, including drug addiction precipitated by an unfaithful first husband. When her current husband (of twenty-eight years) took me to see my sister, she recognized me instantly and gave me a hug. She is well cared for and very happy. She smiled the whole time I was there. The clinic where she is staying is well managed and certified based on an Alzheimer's book titled *I Am Still Here.* Both our mother and grandmother had the same disease. As I was leaving and said goodbye to my sister, I gave her what might be our final hug. As I left the building, I asked God my sister and all the patients be okay.

Shortly after I returned home, my brother-in-law sent me the following:

Since you were here, the Alzheimer's clinic had added three new beneficial features:

1. Started bringing in very beautiful and friendly dogs to visit the residents, which the residents, especially your sister, really loved.

2. Taking the memory-care residents outside the facility for various activities. The first of which was a visit to a beautiful local park; then on the return trip, they stopped at a shop to have ice cream. Again, the residents really enjoyed the timeout.
3. The clinic started preparing and serving healthier meals. I sat with your sister on three occasions, and it was a welcome sight. For example, one meal included fresh-grilled chicken and freshly cooked and nicely seasoned asparagus. I even tried and liked the asparagus. One of the reasons we moved your sister to the clinic was because of the advertised healthy menu selection. Not only advertised, but also we ate there several times before the move and really enjoyed it. But changes occurred, and the nutritionist was released. Food quality declined to packaged and heated products. Lots of complaints caused the clinic to revert back to healthy choices.

Do you suppose my request to God helped? Why and however He did it, it's my judgment we have nothing to lose by asking for his intervention. And look at the gain for all the clinic residents. It is my judgment I was compelled to go so God could feel and share my love for my sister and the others in the clinic. Once He had felt it, do you suppose He was compelled to act? It is my judgment He may need to feel and share our motive for asking before He can act and change the negative effects of free will.

Church Member Experiences with the Ultimate Reality

As told to me by one of our church members, she was napping when her grandchildren came in, looked at her, and ran out to tell their grandfather two people were sleeping with their grandmother. The children tried to describe the two people. When the grandfather went in to look for himself, he didn't see anyone. Sometime after the experience, the whole family went to a church service in a different town. The children excitedly exclaimed two of the statues in the new church were the people sleeping with their grandmother. The two statues were of Mary and Jesus. The whole family now treats the grandmother's religious beliefs and actions with more respect.

A second church member told me an interesting experience she had after her husband passed away. One day she was going through her husband's stocking drawer—one she had been in many times. Unexpectedly, she found a note to her from her late husband. I didn't ask what the note said. I sensed she felt her husband was communicating with her.

Whether you are aware or not, you or someone you know may have encountered events like those above. All one needs to do is learn to recognize interventions and interactions in life as evidence of an ultimate reality. There is a God, a Satan, and life after death.

Our Neighbor's Broken Hip

One day our dog was barking at our neighbor's fence. Our neighbor was eighty-two years old and already had experienced one knee surgery. I opened the back door and called our dog inside. I did not hear our neighbor call my name. Sometime later, the doorbell rang. As my wife put our dog away, I answered the door. There were two members of a religious group soliciting members. As I dismissed them by saying we already attended another church, I noticed a firetruck and an ambulance in front of our house. So I went out and asked the neighbors why the emergency vehicles were there. Our neighbor had fallen in her backyard and broken her hip. Luckily, she had a phone with her and could dial for help. It took her some time to realize she had her phone; she was cold and in shock. I asked the Boss that she be okay. Although she had a hip replacement, she recovered.

At the time, I wondered if God brought the situation to my attention so I could ask for his intersession. This may seem like a stretch, but our doorbell rings only a few times a year. And if I am correct about the metaphysical model God uses in interacting with us, bad things happen to good people without God's intercession unless we ask. When serious events occur, I ask for his intervention.

Several months later, my wife and I left early one fall morning to miss the crowds at the opening of a new warehouse store. We didn't leave early enough—there were no parking places. We returned home. As we drove into our driveway, I noticed the side gate to our neighbor's house was open. While unusual, I didn't think any more about it. I let the dog out of the truck and led him around to our side gate. As I approached our gate, next to our neighbor's gate, I recognized our neighbor's faint voice calling my name. She had fallen again near where she fell before and couldn't get up. She assured us she hadn't broken anything this time, so we helped her up and into her warm house.

What if we hadn't come home early? She could have suffered exposure. This time she had left her phone out of reach. We worried about her living alone, especially since we knew she couldn't get up if she fell. A week and a half later, we noticed she had a cast on her arm. When asked why, she told us she fractured her arm when she fell. It is my judgment we could not find a parking place at the warehouse store because God intervened a second time so we could help her. Our neighbor could have been outside in the cold for several more hours.

Pay attention to the interventions and interruptions in your life. God may be protecting you, your family, and/or your neighbor.

Need to Touch Someone at Church

Shortly after our trip to Europe, my wife and I went to church in a neighboring town so my wife could light a candle and say a prayer at the foot of one of her country's saints. On the way to the neighboring church, I told my wife I had a feeling I needed to touch someone. The feeling was compulsive. While my wife was saying her prayer in church, I saw a young teenager in the pew in front of me. I wondered if he was the one I was supposed to touch. I thought better of any such overt and invasive action. After the service, my wife and I went to the cafeteria for brunch and sat at an empty table. Two couples who apparently did not know each other joined us. None of us introduced ourselves.

As we were finishing, I told them about our trip to Lourdes and the miracle I had experienced. They seemed interested. The husband of one couple said he would like to take his wife there. At that moment, I became aware of an oxygen pump she had to use when she was walking. Her husband explained his wife was too ill to make the trip to Lourdes. After all of us had finished eating, the other two couples stood up to leave. The husband of the second couple reached over and shook my hand. As the ill lady was the last to stand, I reached over with one finger and said, "If I have any grace left, I give it to you." She reached over and, touching my finger with her finger, thanked me. We haven't seen them since. Was this the person I was supposed to touch? I think so.

These events just occurred naturally. It doesn't seem like coincidence I would be compelled to touch someone on the way to church and end up doing so. It never happened before and hasn't happened since. To this day, I still wonder if she is okay. But I really don't need to know. I did what God wanted me to do. But why did He want me to touch someone? Is this kind of experience as important as asking? Maybe.

A Grocery Store Staff Member

Recently as I was going into a grocery store, a young lady, going out to retrieve carts, said, "Thank you." I responded by saying, "You're welcome." I wondered what she was thanking me for. As I left the store, she was coming in. This time she said, "Thank you again!" And again, I said, "You're welcome." Again, I wondered why she was thanking me. I hadn't given her a tip or anything.

On the way home, I remembered the brief discussion the same grocery store lady and I had the previous day. I was at a support counter putting my groceries in bags. She was on the other side. She said, "Good morning." I answered by saying, "Good morning to you," and added, "How are you doing today?" She said, "I am getting by." I responded, "That's good. How is your husband? I saw him with you once." She said, "He is at home just getting by." Privately, I wished her and her husband well, and we parted.

The day she was thanking me, I pondered, "What was the grocery store lady thanking me for?" Coincidently(?), that night, I ran across the following:

> ***Believe me, in the presence of infinite wisdom. One act of humility is worth more than all the knowledge of the world. (St. Teresa of Avila)***

Was the young lady thanking me for just acknowledging her and briefly talking with her? Wow. I can't imagine so few people talk to her. I was just doing something instinctive in me. What is this thing called humility? In my culture, humility is often considered a weakness. Humble people are often not respected and considered easily manipulated and controlled by others. I wonder if that's why some people become narcissistic and prideful. But not talking to another person? Just because I care about others' feelings and respect them doesn't make me think any less of myself. In some way, we are all one in God's eyes. If one wants to be aware of the ultimate reality and directly experience God's love, I would strongly recommend being humble.

The next week the same lady and I exchanged greetings. She was happy. Her smile was contagious. I watched as she talked with and helped two store customers. She certainly was not transparent.

Sometime later she told me about an interesting experience she had regarding her mother. Her mother told her to use her lotto card after she passed away. But the young lady was so upset when her mother did pass away she didn't think about using the lotto card. The lotto card had the winning numbers for the lotto following her mother's death. Wow. Do the deceased have some influence on what happens down here? The odds of such an event happening by chance are virtually zero.

The Homeless Elderly "God Is Great" Lady

One day, after grocery shopping, I was compelled to take a specific exit. As I was approaching the exit, I noticed an elderly lady sitting in a folding chair, holding her cute little dog and a sign asking for help. I managed to pull out a ten-dollar bill and hand it to her without slowing down the exit traffic lane. She thanked me profusely. As she sat back down in her chair, she showed the money to her dog, kissed the bill, and thanked God. She ended by saying "God is great." No wonder I was compelled (by God) to take that specific exit. I wish I had given her more. I ask God to take care of the precious lady. But isn't that what He was doing?

The next day I woke with a question: "Where and by whom are homeless people, like the elderly 'God is great' lady, being taken care of?" Later that morning, I was again compelled to go back to the same grocery store. As I was leaving, there was a gentleman sitting at the exit asking for donations to help feed the poor. I gave him what I could afford. I believe my question earlier that morning was answered. Thank you, God. *We* are all responsible.

The Homeless Man and His Dog

I saw a homeless man and his dog early one morning at a coffee stand and complimented him on his handsome dog. He responded in a rather loud, direct manner, "You're just saying that to make yourself feel good. And there is no God either." I didn't respond. The whole scene reminded me of Mother Teresa's version of the "Anyway Poem": "If you are kind, people may accuse you of selfish, ulterior motives; be kind anyway." The poem concludes with the statement "You see, in the final analysis, it is between you and your God; It was never between you and them anyway." During another encounter, the homeless man told me, "Homeless people need compassion, not sympathy."

At another coincidental meeting, I asked him if he ever felt, what might be considered, God's attempt to help him. The homeless man said yes but "I just didn't pay any attention." God attempts to help all of us. When I look at my own past, I can't count the number of times I failed to act—maybe I was not as aware as I could or should have been.

I met this homeless man a few more times. He and his obviously well-cared-for dog were like one; the dog responded to his owner's slightest gesture. During our brief discussions, he told me about his father and the home he grew up in. When the homeless man was young, he had had a disagreement with another boy (possibly a family relative), and his father suggested both go to the backyard to settle their issues. I don't know if they did or not.

One Sunday morning outside the coffee shop, the homeless man shared his favorite country music with me (played from his cell phone loudly through two backpack speakers). As I sat outside on the grocery store bench, he stood up, sang, and danced to the music. He must have played fifteen or more songs. After each, he told me all about the song's and vocalist's histories. Passing people had smiles on their faces. It was an interesting and delightful experience. The homeless man and his dog were happy. So was I for having met them. As I left, I asked God they be okay.

A Homeless Man Just Looking for Work

One day when I was sitting outside a local coffee shop enjoying my coffee and the beautiful morning, an apparent homeless man sat down beside me with a sign that read "Need a Job." He told me he had worked at a local recreation vehicle dealership. They closed it and moved to another town. He was one of many employees the dealership did not transfer. He had been self-sufficient up to that point. Apparently, he had no spouse or children. When he failed to quickly find a new position, he was forced to live with his brother during the winter months but had to live out of his truck during the summer. His social services income was barely enough to meet his immediate needs.

He became very depressed and had sought help from a local suicide prevention organization. They asked him if he had any weapons at home. He admitted he had a pistol for protection. When he refused to turn it over, the organization apparently told the police. I am not certain, but apparently, in his condition and maybe something in his past, it was a felony for him to own a weapon. The police seized the weapon and arrested him on a felony charge. The court overthrew the felony charge, but apparently his arrest remained on his record. Previously, when he had been on the street with his sign, a local businessman had stopped, gave him his business card, and told him to come in the following week for an interview. When he went in for an interview, the businessman was no longer interested. When the homeless man asked why, the businessman said, "You have too much baggage."

Apparently, the above events were recent. I offered him some money, but he refused. He said, "I am not looking for handouts. I am looking for work." As we parted, he went back out to the street with his sign. As I walked to my car, I asked God to help this man find a job and be okay. I haven't seen the man since.

The Note

One day when I was getting coffee at a coffee stand, I found a handwritten note beside the sugar and cream. In summary, the note someone had made for themselves said "Pray—I am not God; Write daily—Poems(?); Acknowledge good effort, not outcome; Live in the moment; Anxiety push to the future; Fear push to the past; Read!" I could not decipher the author's name.

How interesting. I couldn't have said it better. It's my judgment this experience was not coincidence. This experience was both a push and a pull to work on this book and share my experiences just as the above note's author had done for me. Don't shy away from sharing your experiences and views with others. And don't succumb to Satan's use of fear. Accept anxiety as a gentle push from the Boss. And for heaven's sake, read. Later in this book, I give examples of why reading is so important. It's one way God interacts with us.

V

Asks

Ask, and it will be given to you. Seek, and you will find. Knock, and it will be opened for you. For everyone who asks receives. He who seeks finds. To him who knocks it will be opened.
—Matthew 7

24. Asks for a Son

My youngest son is very sensitive; he has a big heart. Animals seem to literally attach themselves to him. When he lived in a trailer next to a friend's house, a small newly hatched bird had fallen out of its nest. For some reason, it jumped up on the front of my son's shoe and wouldn't leave. My son picked it up but was unable to return it to its nest. He drove around town looking for an animal shelter that would help the little bird. When he finally found one, they said they couldn't take it. When one of the senior employees came out and asked if the little bird was sick, my son hesitated but finally understood he had to say it was sick before they could accept the little bird.

In another experience, a dog from across the busy road came over to my son's trailer—apparently driven by curiosity or some other sense. My son and the dog apparently shared an ephemeral moment because the dog would come over and sleep on my son's trailer's step waiting for my son to wake up. The dog's owner asked my son if he wanted to keep the dog, but my son declined. My son never saw the dog again. The owner apparently took the dog to an animal shelter. My son has had like experiences with other animals, including horses. It is my judgment that animals can see or feel something with certain humans. Maybe it's a type of agape love. One thing is for sure, God has a hand in it. Unfortunately, our culture's logical, rational, prudent way of thinking seems to dismiss out of hand intuition and emotions (empathy, love, and sorrow).

When my son was nine years old attending a local grade school, he noticed a group of students harassing a minority student. He stepped right in and defended the minority student. The principal of the school had me called at work, threatening to suspend my son for fighting. Apparently, the other boys weren't being punished. I was furious. After I threatened legal action against the school district, the whole issue, apparently, was dropped. I was proud of my son for defending his fellow student.

One day, many years later, as I was passing the area where my young son lived, I was worried about his well-being. And as parents sometimes do, I asked God to give him a girlfriend (for company and purpose) and help him find a way to make a better living. God responded. Within a short time, my son had his own business (he was making more money than me) and a girlfriend. I thought all was well. Within two years, he had lost his business. He was deeply in debt. I couldn't believe it. What had happened?

In short, an out-of-state competitor moved in and took over his customers. His girlfriend wanted to marry him, but he hesitated. Eventually, she left.

What went wrong here? First, I asked for the wrong things. Be careful what you ask for. In this case, I needed to simply ask that my son be okay and not superimpose my value system on his life. Presently, my son is taking care of his invalid mother and stepfather. He certainly has meaningful responsibilities. Maybe that's what God had in store for him all along. I am and will always be proud of him—an exceptionally sensitive, just soul. Help your children find their own way. Be patient, kind, loving, helpful, and understanding.

25. World Leader Requests

And now for some of my biggest requests. I am sure many others gave God their input. What's interesting? They all occurred within a short time of when I asked. Coincidence? Unlikely. Maybe, in each case, my justification was in consonance with His ethos (character, fundamental values). Because of free will, He needs us to ask, freeing Him to act.

Four World Leaders

Prior to the following experience, I saw a news report on a young college-educated Tunisian father of three young children who committed suicide in a Tunisian city park by burning himself to death. Why did he commit suicide? Apparently, he was unable to support his family (wife and three small children) selling apples in a local park. The story so upset me I went to my world globe and asked God to remove, what I perceived to be, three self-aggrandized leaders from three countries. I presented arguments on why each of the three were, in some way, evil, and, as always, surrendered to His will. I was shocked to learn a short time later that one of the leaders had died in his sleep that night, one had been killed within a few days, and later the third had been hung following a revolution. Apparently, God agreed with my request and all the other requests I am sure He received.

The US 2016 presidential election was certainly indicative of a divided society. The consequences of such a politically divided society, as existed in Germany in the early 1930s, could lead to a society so interested in avoiding near-term conflict through appeasement, we could end up in another world war. Few knew after Neville Chamberlin of the United Kingdom, Edouard Daladier of France, and Adolf Hitler signed the Munich accord in 1938, Hitler, when asked by a subordinate why he signed the agreement, didn't answer. He simply threw his copy in the trash. The trusting Allies were not prepared for the coming war that cost the world at least fifty million lives. Thank goodness Franklin D. Roosevelt started preparing the US for World War II before we were attacked. By the end of the war, the US had one hundred aircraft carriers and over one hundred battleships at sea or being built. Prior to the United States 2016 presidential election, I asked God for a "strong president," respectful of human rights and freedom across the world—one who had the will and ability to prepare for anything. So far, the result looks okay. Only time will tell.

The Pope

One day when I was pondering the death of Pope St. John Paul II long after he passed, I felt the world needed a more unconventional leader of the world's largest Christian religion. I decided to ask God for a pope who would unite humanity with a less orthodox, more personal supreme being and fix some of the church's subordinate and financial problems. I wanted a pope who would be sensitive to differing world cultures, religions, and ethnic heritages. I wanted a pope who would be more aware of how the ultimate realities of God, Satan, and those in the hereafter interact directly with each of us. Shortly after I asked, I heard the present pope was retiring—something that hadn't happened in six hundred years. Sometime after Pope Francis assumed his new position, I understand the previous pope said God asked him to retire. What does this experience mean? Does God really listen to our suggestions and act? Surely He knows what's going on down here. Maybe free will prevents Him from acting solely on how He would like people to act and behave. So? Ask Him. And tell Him why you're asking. Asking seems to be an important way of praying.

26. Other Asks

CTA Scans

Before I retired, I needed to make certain my health was still okay before I gave up my benefits. I was not feeling well and needed a break from work. The symptoms I was experiencing could have been caused by a lung or heart condition. Because of my family history and my lifetime of high cholesterol, my doctor sent me to the local university medical center for a sixty-four-slice computer tomography angiogram (CTA). Knowing there was a high probability they would find more than one problem, I was very nervous about knowing. My father had heart surgery when he was a few years younger than I was at the time.

After the CTA, the university doctor took me into the computer analysis room and showed me the results of the first few slices. He explained how the scan could show heart problems not detectable in a normal angiogram. The final image, which would take some time to develop, would show my heart pumping in three dimensions from any aspect to virtually any depth.

As I was driving to the doctor's office to get the results of the CTA, I asked God to see that I was okay. This time, I got no immediate perceptible response. The doctor gave me a copy of both the CT and CTA scan results and started the review by saying everything was normal. My first thoughts were *What does normal mean? How much blockage do I have? I must have some.* The doctor then said, "Your heart is normal sized with no plaque or calcification." One artery was 50 percent smaller than normal, but healthy.

I couldn't believe it. At my age with my family history, the results were profound. Many men have some plaques by the time they are in their late twenties. Apparently, my symptoms were caused by being overweight, lack of exercise, and stress. My conclusion? The Boss must still have something he wanted me to do.

A Football Game

A friend once told me God doesn't do wars and football games. His comment ended our friendlier discussions. The following occurred more than a year earlier.

One Sunday my wife and I were watching the end of a local football league playoff game. There were only a few seconds left on the clock. The opposition had the ball near the local team's goal and was ready to kick a three-pointer. If they were successful, they would win. To prove to myself there are requests God won't answer, just before the snap, I turned to my wife and told her I had just asked God to help our team win—a seeming impossibility. Then the ball was snapped. The opposition's quarterback fumbled the ball. He picked it up and tried to run it around the left side of his line. He failed and fumbled the ball a second time. Our team recovered the ball and won the game. I will never forget the amazed look on my wife's face. I was very surprised. I never expected God to respond. Maybe it was just coincidence. This was one of the most direct and unlikely responses I have ever asked for. What were the odds the other higher-ranked team would fail? One in a hundred? But then, what were the odds they would fail the one time I asked? Thousands of people root for their home teams play by play. Did He listen to me this time? Maybe it had something to do with encouraging me to ask more often.

Stock Market

It had been almost six weeks since I had started playing a major television network's stock market contest. I wasn't doing well at all—I think I had made 5 percent. What's worse, I had read the rules several times, watched the market using many different tools, and monitored (more like marveled at) how the weekly winners were able to make 50 to 80 percent gains in their portfolios. I also noticed by midweek that several names were often repeated on the leader list. I assumed the multiple listing of names was a coincidence. Finally, early one morning I was walking my dog when I realized I didn't even know how to play the game. In my frustration, I told God, "I sense there is no way I am going to win anything in the contest." All I wanted was to know how to play the game. It was clear one had to use a completely different strategy than if you were playing with real money. Did you have to risk it all with each investment? It was my judgment that's what the winners were doing. In retrospect, I think some players may have had insider information on certain stocks.

I don't remember how I found out, but within a day I realized the multiple names on the weekly winner list were not a coincidence. Contestants could have more than one portfolio. Since the rules didn't explicitly state multiple portfolios were allowed, I assumed they weren't. So I immediately signed up ten more portfolios and began selecting stocks. I spent four days studying potential buyout candidates and stocks with earnings reports due out the following week. I included only stocks that had histories of large percentage changes following earnings reports, something I would never do with real money or a single portfolio. By the weekend, I felt I had done my homework. I was ready for Monday trading.

On Monday morning, I went immediately into my home office and pulled up the stock market contest page. One of my stocks, which I put into three portfolios, had gone up 18 percent in the first hour. Wow! I had made more in one hour than I had in six weeks with one portfolio. By Wednesday I had made 31 percent in two portfolios. I was over 50 percent in one portfolio, and it was only midweek.

Then I blew it. The last hour of Wednesday trading, rather than hold the day's winning stock one more day, I decided to buy a different stock with earnings coming out after the market close. As I was trying to buy the stock twenty minutes before the close, my doorbell rang three times and the phone twice, a virtual impossibility. Somehow, even with all the interruptions, I managed to buy the new stock—I put the whole portfolio into it. If I had stayed in the stock I had owned on Wednesday, I would have made 10 percent more on Thursday. And if, and if…? I didn't win the week. But I had made over 63 percent, more than most previous weekly winners. And I had figured out how to play the game. Thanks, Boss! So why the sudden change in fortune? I think it was the combination of asking how to play the game and doing a massive amount of homework (I picked the right stocks, but the combination across the eleven portfolios was not optimum).

If I had not changed stocks on Wednesday and made my original planned buy for Friday, I might have won the week. I think God helped me develop the plan. So what happened? I wondered if all the interruptions I got on Wednesday twenty minutes before the close were God's attempt to interrupt and stop me from changing stocks. I go weeks with maybe two or three doorbell and phone interruptions. All the calls were legitimate; I had to take them. For the rest of the contest, if I planned to buy or sell a stock or an option and I got interrupted by anything, even our dog's barking, I didn't make the trade. How did it work out? I didn't make much play money. But I didn't lose any either. And I learned how to play the game.

My Son's Near Car Crash

I was worried when I found out one of my sons had a serious infection across two of his molars. He was in great pain, and they could not be treated for a week. Over-the-counter medication and an antibiotic didn't help. He was sick enough there was some risk he might have to be rushed to the hospital. I asked God to take care of him. I did not want to lose my son.

I later took him to a university dental clinic where he was successfully treated. It was interesting, however, that a few days later he was visiting friends. When he decided to leave, one of the host's children ran out to his car and asked him to stay longer. They played catch for a few minutes, and then my son left. On the way home, he was stopped at a major accident that had occurred just a few minutes earlier. He believes he could have been involved if he had left earlier as planned. Did asking God my son to be okay affect not only his health but also his life? Maybe.

You have nothing to lose by asking God to take care of family members and others. He shares your love for them.

The Weather on a Cruise

Several years ago, my family went on an ocean cruise to Alaska. It was grand. I hope someday we can do it again. We went in May when the rates were cheapest. As I was planning our itinerary at the various stops, I noticed we were scheduled to visit North America's largest and wettest rainforest. Although most months are rainy, May was normally one of the wettest. Since we were spending a significant amount of time and money on this trip, I was more than just a little anxious about the weather. Before we left, I asked that it not rain. Not one raindrop fell on us. Not even at sea. Misty? Yes, but no rain.

A Significant Work Project

I had a dream once of leading the development of a US Navy Littoral Autonomous Systems Network (LASN) comprised of a dozen small stingray-shaped autonomous undersea robots. I developed the concept while representing a university laboratory on a US Navy Undersea Warfare Committee. With support from several naval research laboratories, a Navy program executive officer, and an undersecretary of defense, I almost got the project funded until 9/11. So with the support of the project's advocates, I attempted to get the project funded via a congressional budget plus up. After being told the project was going to be submitted, I waited anxiously until the defense budget had been passed. I monitored the congressional websites for several days and nights. The one key congressional website was offline—I couldn't get resolution on the project's status. One morning I got up at three o'clock and went to the key website—it was still offline. After two hours, I finally told God it was okay if the project didn't get funded. By doing so, I let His will prevail. Within a second of making that mental statement, the site came online. You guessed it—the project was not funded. I was terribly disappointed. But He let me say it was okay before He told me. He does that a lot. Apparently, when I finally surrender to His will, He is gentle but resolved.

Young Lady at a University Medical Center

My son asked me to drive him to a university dental clinic to have two teeth extracted. Both were infected and had been for over a year. If he required oral surgery, they would put him immediately into an operating room. He didn't have insurance, but the costs at the medical center were affordable.

Since I was in the middle of starting this book, I believed some things were not coincidence. I wondered what the Boss had in store for us. It was a costly day in both time and money. Since we got to the medical center early, my son wanted to smoke one last cigarette. We walked all over the hospital looking for a place to smoke. We found a smoking room. After we were there for a few minutes, we started talking to a young lady in a wheelchair. She looked to be in her early twenties. She told us her life story. She was at the hospital to get off heroin and other drugs. She was homeless, living under a freeway overpass. She had no family except a brother in Massachusetts. Her brother wouldn't have anything to do with her. In summary, she seemed hopelessly lost. No purpose or meaning in her life except to get high. She told us what it was like to be homeless, to be constantly robbed, beaten, and worse. She was very gaunt and did not look healthy.

My son's and my suggestions seemed trite. We didn't know what to say, yet we felt the need to say something hopeful. My son suggested she get new friends or go live with a friend for a while. I was going to tell her to ask God for help, but I didn't think she would give it a second thought. I regret not telling her anyway. I told her when I was eleven years old I asked my mother about drugs. My mother responded by asking me, "What are the things you enjoy doing the most?" I answered as any eleven-year-old boy might. I said, "Fishing, building train sets, reading, and building models." My mother then told me, "If you use drugs, you will never do any of those things again." The impact of my mother's statement has lasted my entire life.

Both my son and I sensed our suggestions of staying away from the drug crowd and focusing on doing things one likes to do were too little too late for this young lady. As we walked away, I told my son I had asked God to help her. He said he had done the same. We sensed she needed to talk about her life. Maybe we did help her feel better even if only for a moment. I wish I knew how this story ended. And then again, maybe not.

Several weeks after this experience, I had an epiphany. Maybe this young lady's story had more meaning for my son and me than we realized. I looked at my own life to see if I was doing the things I enjoyed most. Instantly I realized I was not. Many years ago, I took my stepson to a medical specialist. On his office wall, the doctor had a poster showing a family watching TV. The poster had the caption "The Drug of Choice." I suggest "drugs" can be interpreted as including life's baser distractions that, if taken to excess, can prevent us from living. With that understanding, "drugs" could include TV, alcohol, nicotine, carnality, and many others. Actions and states of mind that distract us from being joyful can cause depression, apathy, a sense of unhappiness, poor physical health, anger, loneliness (even the fear of being alone), frustration, and, in general, take away from our quality of life. I suspect this issue contributes to the increase in national suicides. Some very successful and famous people have committed suicide (Ernest Hemingway, Robin Williams, Anthony Bourdain, and many others).

What other kinds of traps can one fall into that take from the quality of our lives? If a person is raised by a parent who celebrated only achievements, that person may find they are constantly waiting for the next big achievement to give their life meaning and fulfillment. Big achievements are far and few between. Instead of enjoying every day and sharing love and life's beauty with others, such a person is subject to suffering constant depression and exaggerated self-esteem. Who we are and how we choose to live may be one of life's great purposes. Because we have free will, we must make choices daily. Do so wisely. Ask God for help. Smile and relish moments spent with others. Your choices may determine who and what you become, not just in this life, but the next as well.

Lady at a Grocery Store

One day on the way home from work, I stopped at a local store to get gas and a bottle of wine. One cashier was dealing with a lotto customer. As I stood at the end of a second line, I glanced over at an older lady cashing in her lotto tickets. I had seen her walking to and from the store many times. This activity was probably a central part of her life. A sense of compassion overwhelmed me. I asked God to let her win. At that very moment, I heard the cashier tell her she had won three times her money. This type of response happens so often in my life it has forced me to take note. Even though I may never know the outcome of such a request, I am compelled to ask.

State Services Position

The following is an experience I thought important enough to include in this book. The lessons I learned were meaningful.

My largest project at my current employer was coming to an end. I needed to act quickly since jobs were scarce. I sent out a dozen resumes. I had a few interesting interviews, one in particular—an information technology manager position in one of the largest state agencies. As I was driving to the first of two interviews, I told God I wanted the position. The position would have carried me well into my retirement years. Shortly after the first interview, I was asked to return for a second interview with the agency's senior managers. Only two applicants were being considered.

Two months passed with no letter and no phone call. I had since been selected for a part-time position at my previous employer. One day I was curious about what happened with the state position. I had heard the agency was in serious upheaval. The senior manager had been replaced. Remembering I had not consciously subordinated my will to His, I told God that it was okay if I hadn't been selected. That afternoon, I received a letter in the mail indicating I had not been selected. The timing was interesting. The letter had been sent before I surrendered to His will. Does He know what we are going to choose? Does He go back in time and change events? Does He put thoughts into our minds? In retrospect, I think things worked out as they were supposed to. And I don't think His time base and ours are the same.

Apparently, the job was not God's plan for me. I remember wondering, "What is His plan for me?" The book I had been thinking about since I was nineteen? Whatever. He wanted me working only part-time.

The Lady Store Clerk

One day when I went to the local grocery store and sat outside with my coffee and a cigarette, one of the store clerks joined me on the bench. Somehow, we started talking about this book. As we sat there, I told her three experiences I was writing about at the time. One was about the Voice, another was about a miracle I experienced in Europe, and the third was about a college paper on how and why the Cold War would end without an all-out World War III. As she went through about five cigarettes listening to the above three experiences, I explained some would say the experiences were examples of what a mystic, a saint, and a prophet might experience. I explained a friend felt those terms were too much to put into a book. As I retrieved a new pack of cigarettes from my car and returned to the bench, she said, "You really need to include those terms in your book." We talked for a minute or two, and she returned to her job. I felt bad because she probably used both of her breaks. But rethinking our discussion, I decided to include those terms in this paragraph. It's my judgment those experiences occurred at moments when I was in a high state of grace. They certainly helped me become aware of the ultimate reality, an opportunity you also have.

A Snowstorm

One fall afternoon after I retired and was driving home from the grocery store, I realized I missed the heavy snowstorms I grew up with in Colorado. Just as I turned toward home, I asked God for a snowstorm of at least one and a half feet—a very unusual and unlikely depth. Since none was forecast, I didn't really give it a second thought. The next morning, we woke up to, you guessed it, snow well over one foot deep. Since we didn't have a four-wheel-drive vehicle, we were snowbound for at least two days. Our godson's parents were still able to drop him off at our house since they had a four-wheel-drive vehicle. My wife and I, our godson, and our dog had a great time playing in the snow. A coincidence? Not likely. Sometimes He seems to give us the small things we ask for.

The Mouse

A few years ago, I found a dead mouse in the garage in a closed trap. I carelessly hadn't checked the trap in over a week. As was my original plan, I took the trap out behind our back fence and inadvertently dropped the mouse on a bed of blackberry bushes full of thorns. It didn't move. It was so small and precious. I couldn't help asking God to bring it back to life. I told Him there were no witnesses and, therefore, no one's free will would be violated. I then reached down and gently touched the mouse with my right forefinger. It instantly jumped a foot in the air and ran off into the bushes. Apparently, God agreed with my request.

27. Ask Summary

I ask often, sometimes daily. Just a few ask experiences are included in this book. Sometimes I ask for the wrong thing, in the wrong way, or for the wrong reason. Other times I fail to understand His response. Sometimes I get a delayed or no response. That's okay.

I don't expect Him to always answer. My goal is to free Him so He can act independently of the "free will" law that governs humanity's relationship with the ultimate reality. I always leave the actual results in His hands—He has many others to consider. I believe asking, especially for others, is the most powerful way of praying. If you have surrendered to His will, no response is a response.

Postscript: Recently, He seems to answer my requests virtually in real time. Sometimes, I suspect, even prompting me to ask. Maybe I am getting better at interpreting when to ask and how He answers.

VI

Jesus

28. A Sad Newspaper Article

I was drawn to a newspaper story on the suicide death of Chris Cornell in 2017 stating his wife could not listen to his band's music or bear the sound of his voice. Per Wikipedia, Chris was ranked fourth in the list of "Heavy Metal's All-Time Top 100 Vocalists" by *Hit Parador*, ninth in the list of "Best Lead Singers of All Time" by *Rolling Stone*, and nominated for fifteen Grammy awards, winning twice. Chris's widow released a statement for the press stating, "Many of us who knew Chris well noticed that he wasn't himself during his final hours and that something was very off." Apparently, he lived a life of depression and substance abuse. After many years of sobriety, the autopsy report revealed "several substances were found in his system." He was buried at the Hollywood Forever Cemetery.

I found his 2008 television interview statement about religion interesting. He said,

> I don't follow any particular one…Ultimately, I think I am sort of a freethinker and kind of open… So many bad things—as well as good things—based on people just sort of blindly following religion that I kind of feel like I want to stay away from any type of specific denomination or any religion, period. If for no other reason

> than just that. I don't want to be involved with anything or condone any school of thought that at some point and in some way causes the death of innocent people… Like the life, for example, of Jesus is well-documented. It's corroborated by different people, who had different backgrounds, and different levels of education. And they wrote about it. We know that this guy existed, and we know pretty much what he said, and it's simple…be really nice to each other and everything will be okay.

The development of a personal relationship with God and awareness of Satan's presence and methods may have helped Chris as well as others considering suicide. Maybe he didn't know about the power of asking. Some of my observations of formal orthodox religions are in consonance with Chris's views. But Chris's summary statement on Jesus is true. If he had time to know Jesus personally as did some of my acquaintances (whose experiences are summarized in the next section), he may have had a much better chance of being at peace with life. Awareness of the ultimate reality at a personal level supersedes all religious dictates. It is the perspective that Jesus taught the disciples and the view ultimately recognized by St. Paul the apostle. Need proof? Research the history of Saul of Tarsus's transition to St. Paul the apostle.

History is full of accomplished adults who were unable to fully adapt to their culture. Van Gogh, a religious man, is one who comes to mind. Apparently, God wanted him to paint. Yet in Van Gogh's lifetime he only sold one painting. Now look at the worth of Van Gogh's paintings—far more than just money.

29. Direct Interactions with Jesus

The Cross

Late in life I bought a cross and chain to wear around my neck, something I had never done before. I bought one with a dove in place of Jesus. I couldn't stand the thought of Jesus suffering on the cross. However, I could never keep the cross from catching on my clothes. And I could never determine what was causing the problem—there were no sharp edges. Eventually, I bought one with Jesus on the cross. Yes, it had edges. I have been wearing it for decades without it ever catching on a single piece of clothing. Is it possible Jesus wanted me to accept his suffering as having some very significant purpose? I think so. And what might that purpose be? By doing so, he saved all of us. On our final judgment day, will He be our lawyer regardless of whether we practiced any formal religion(s)? I think so.

The Tau

Without knowing why, the tau letter (similar in shape to a cross) keeps appearing in my life. My interactions include observing a high cloud formation identical to a tau that formed as I stood outside pondering writing this book. My son saw it and agreed it was a tau. The cloud formation kept its shape as it moved across the evening sky. What caused the exact shape? Why didn't it dissipate or change shape over time? All the cloud formations I have seen do change shape and/or dissipate as they cross the sky.

Just before a church meeting at my home, something (a slug?) left a clear tau symbol on my dining-room sliding door. Curiosities like these don't seem like just coincidences. The tau apparently is the first letter on the first-century ossuaries in the Talpiot Tomb. It is also the symbol St. Francis of Assisi used in signing his correspondence. Apparently, there seems to be special significance to the letter. It may have preceded the cross as a Christian symbol by almost three hundred years. I now have a large tau-like cross with a barbed-wire crown hung over my home office door.

The "I Love You" Card

During one of my outside morning meditations, I was considering the format and outline for this book. I came in to get something from my study, and as I was headed back outside, I noticed a small two-by-three-inch card with "I Love You" stenciled on it lying directly in my path. I didn't see it when I came in the house and down the hall. I knew we had two such cards, but I did not know where they were. How did the card suddenly appear right in my path at that moment? Was it placed there by Jesus? This book is, in large part, due to such seemingly small unlikely experiences. I have kept the card for many years on my desk where I can see it every day.

The Homeless Man—An Apparition?

During the period in my life when I was commuting a long distance to work, I frequently saw a homeless man who looked like the image in the Shroud of Turin without the crucifixion wounds. When the homeless man was standing by the road, I would give him what I could afford. Once, while eating breakfast in a local restaurant, he came up to me and asked for a cigarette. I gave him one. When I left, I gave him the rest of my pack (only one or two cigarettes were left).

I remember he had no food, drink, or anything in front of him, not a menu or place setting. I never saw anyone else interact with him or even acknowledge the man's presence, not even with just a glance.

Years later, I wondered if I had witnessed an apparition of Jesus. Regardless, I regret not leaving the gentleman money for His breakfast. Now I cannot pass a homeless or needy person without giving them what I can afford. For over a decade, I never gave the experience any further thought. After all, the gentleman smoked. Or did He? I never actually saw Him smoke. Later in life, I found by sharing a cigarette with homeless people, I was able to gain an understanding of who they were and why they were homeless. After years of such direct experiences and asking God to see they were okay, I rethought about this first homeless man experience. Maybe he really was an apparition of Jesus, motivating me to do just what I have been doing. It seems like a stretch, but what the heck. It's my judgment today it was an apparition of Jesus teaching me to share God's love for the homeless. If I remember correctly, there have been a few saints who gave up comfortable lives to care for the homeless (e.g., St. Francis of Assisi, St. Ignatius of Loyola, and I am sure many more).

30. Acquaintance Experiences

A Young Boy's Experience

I'll call him Fred. Fred was raised in a Central American country. At a very early age, his father beat him unmercifully. He hid under the kitchen table to avoid daily beatings. His older sister sometimes climbed under the table and beat him. He just stayed under the table and went somewhere else in his head. The consequences? He lives with post-traumatic stress disorder (PTSD) apparently, in part due to his childhood trauma. His PTSD apparently can be triggered by any seemingly unrelated emotional trauma. One day, under the table, Jesus appeared to him and said, "I am always with you." Since then, the young man told me, whenever he feels a PTSD event coming on, the thought of Jesus gives him peace. He doesn't need miracles or the Voice. Ever since he had the apparition, he is comforted by the love of his rescuer—Jesus. The last few times I have seen him he is doing well.

Treat your children with love and kindness. Both Hitler and Stalin were beaten into comas by their stepfather or father. What were the consequences? We all know them well.

A Coworker's Experience

A close friend and coworker told me about the experiences he and his family had with their Christian church. Apparently, the pastor was telling them how to live their lives and he (the pastor) would be the judge of whether they were doing so or not. Also, the pastor demanded a significant percentage of their income to support the church, and of course, his family. One day my friend heard a *voice* tell him to leave that church. It was his belief that he had heard the voice of Jesus. After all, the pastor was supposedly presenting and representing Jesus. Religious authority has been used for centuries to control and manipulate populations for personal gain and power. Maybe the US forefathers were influenced, even compelled, by the good side of the ultimate reality to build a new country. The French and the American colonialists shared the view that each person was endowed, by the Creator, with inalienable rights. The Marquis de Lafayette said someday the US would save the world. Maybe he had a premonition something like World War II would occur.

A Young Lady's Experience

I met a young lady at a friend's house during a party. She shared her traumatic life experiences with me. She was adopted as a child into a family with ten other children—some also adopted. Some of her siblings died at young ages—one hung himself when he was only in his teens. Two other family members passed away during the following year. She married and had two sons. Reluctantly, she had to give up shared custody of her two young sons because of a drug problem. Her drug problem led to a direct encounter with Jesus (I didn't ask the details). And consequently, she became a Catholic. She loves her church and Jesus. She wears His cross around her neck. She has a new adorable son and nice, hardworking husband but still fears going back to drugs. Jesus was and is her salvation. After we parted, I asked God that she be okay. I may never know the end of this story. I suspect the results will be a consequence of a battle between God and Satan. Obviously, free will is a blessing, but one that comes with the responsibility to act in accordance with God's will for us—no small task.

31. Was Jesus Married?

One afternoon driving home from work, I wondered and hoped Jesus had a chance to experience a normal life before he started his mission. I wondered if Jesus had been married and whether or not He had any children. When I got home, I was compelled to watch an interesting movie: *The Da Vinci Code*. It is my understanding the author wrote the book based on extensive research. In summary, the story suggested Jesus was married to Mary Magdalene and they had at least one child. It's my sense that seeing the movie shortly after I asked the question was not coincidence.

The question still lingered. Later, I saw a TV show (produced by a famous Hollywood producer) on what has become known as the "Talpiot Tomb." The tomb was a first-century Jewish family tomb with remains contained in limestone boxes called "ossuaries." Apparently, the Talpiot Tomb contained ossuaries for Mary Magdalene (which would not have been in the tomb unless she was married to one of Jesus's family members), Mother Mary, Jesus, and other family members. The only member not named was St. Joseph, which would have been the case since he died before Jesus started his mission and was probably buried somewhere else. The ossuaries had names etched in Arabica from right to left, starting with a tau symbol. One ossuary was missing, the one belonging to St. James, Jesus's half brother. The missing ossuary was apparently found years later and confirmed when the patina (dust chemical composition unique to each tomb) matched the patina in the other Talpiot Tomb ossuaries (2017). The patina in the Talpiot Tomb is unique. There were also children's ossuaries in the tomb.

An estimate of the probability that the tomb is Jesus's family tomb was 600 to 1 prior to the discovery and testing of the St. James ossuary. With the St. James ossuary, the probability the tomb is Jesus's family tomb increases to 30,000 to 1. Sixty percent of the Talpiot Tomb ossuaries had inscriptions compared to only 20 percent of the other ossuaries found in Israel. The Talpiot Tomb has a partially discernable symbol over the entry that my wife interprets as "under this roof lies the light of the world." Maybe, when it was carved, it was supposed to look like that today. Apparently, the tomb lies close to (may even be part of) property belonging to St. Joseph of Arimathea, the wealthy pharisee who, according to all four conical gospels, took possession of Jesus's body after the crucifixion. The use of an ossuary holding only bones is consistent with the placement of Jesus's body somewhere else for a year or more while His body decayed (like the Church of the Holy Sepulcher?). And who knows, maybe there were never any bones in the Jesus ossuary. It's up to you to believe or not believe the Talpiot Tomb was Jesus's family tomb. It's my belief it is Jesus's family tomb.

After stumbling on to these two movies after I had questions about Jesus's life between twelve and thirty, his death, and possible marriage to St. Mary Magdalene, it doesn't seem logical being compelled to watch these two shows was just coincidence. My intuition says Jesus was married to Mary Magdalene and they may have had at least one child. This whole issue of His bone ossuary existing is consistent with at least one of the Gnostic Gospels—the gospel according to Peter where witnesses say Jesus's spirit was escorted into heaven by two angels.

The Shroud of Turin, apparently *a negative image* of someone who died on the cross with the same wounds Jesus suffered, may well be confirmation Jesus's rise to heaven was at least, in some sense, a supernatural event. The fact that His bones might have remained on earth doesn't change my acceptance of Jesus as the Messiah. After all, I have had direct experiences with Him in my life, and so have you, whether you are *aware* of them or not. He did rise! I don't find the concept of how Jesus rose from dead taking anything away from my love for Him. Rather, experiences like those in this book answer my questions and only add to my awareness. And now, St. Mary Magdalene has been added to my list of heroines. Even Gandhi said he had no problem with Jesus. Don't let the academia or religious orthodoxy change how you feel about Jesus. He existed and, whether you are aware or not, is with you every day.

As an aside, since Jesus might have been married, priests who want to marry might be able to become deacons. Since marriage is a normal human state, maybe fewer priests would leave the church altogether (about 150 leave every year in the United States). I have been told priests guilty of abuse can't be changed. No doubt about it, the Pope has some tough problems to fix. I ask God to help him.

VII

Precognitions

*When you experience events
that appear to be just coincidence, think again.*

32. A Prophecy

In my first year at college, a political science teacher asked us to write a paper on how the Cold War would end; were we headed to World War III? My paper started with an assessment of the consequences of a full-out nuclear exchange between the United States and the Soviet Union. After researching the possibilities, I discussed an exchange based on the Soviet Union's strategic nuclear weapons and our smaller tactical nuclear weapons. It would have taken only eight Soviet weapons and the accompanying fires to significantly reduce oxygen levels over the Northern Hemisphere, taking more than ten minutes to recover a significant percentage of the oxygen—a long time considering how fast oxygen diffuses. The research was based on articles in several news magazines. My paper took the position that such an exchange would end civilization in both countries and be an environmental catastrophe for the whole world. Certainly the leaderships knew. Then why the constant threats?

I then predicted something unimaginable at the time (1964). I predicted the Bear (the Soviet Union) would not be our enemy in a potential World War III. Our greatest threat was more likely to be China. Why? Because of their population size and agrarian society, they could take a significant population loss without suffering complete collapse—in my opinion, something the US could not do. One of the main points of the assignment was how to avoid World War III. My answer was to integrate the Chinese and US economies. Though our professor didn't necessarily agree with my views, I was one of only two people asked to read their paper to the whole class. Another viewpoint I expressed in the paper was, "America was the melting pot of the world," a view Hitler felt was America's greatest weakness.

It's interesting that many decades later, the end of the Cold War in 1989 and the integration of our economy with China are as I predicted. At the time, I didn't know then where the idea came from. I know now. All prophecies come from God! I remember writing about the rate of technology change favoring a *free society*. In today's world, ideas and a technology base can be stolen before they're even put into practice. Maybe, in the long term, only human empathetic morality and a strong intolerance for self-focused evil agendas can save us as a species. If humanity fails, the Bible's Armageddon prediction may come to pass sooner than it would otherwise. In an ever-changing world, it's up to humanity to work hard for good causes and to defend all cultures against evil.

33. Direct Precognitions

The First Precognition

I had heard of precognitions but, quite frankly, didn't believe in them. As I glanced up at a highway sign in the 1970s while driving to work one morning, I saw thin black graffiti lines covering a highway sign. As I focused on the sign, the lines disappeared. I thought I must have something under my contacts. I didn't. As I approached the second highway sign, I saw the same type of graffiti. It also disappeared as I approached. It was like that all the way to my work exit. Really weird. Once at work, I simply forgot the whole thing. I didn't think about the experience again until two days later.

Two days later on the way to work, I saw the exact same graffiti on the first overpass highway sign. This time, the thin black lines did not disappear. Again, the graffiti existed on all the signs up to my work exit sign. The nightly news reported someone, probably in an elevated cherry picker, had sprayed thin black graffiti on all the highway signs very early in the morning. Police were investigating. I don't know if the perpetrators were ever caught.

A friend told me this type of experience is called a precognition. I told a few family members about the experience but forgot it almost as soon as it happened. I didn't sense the experience was spiritual. I am certain it was real. So what are these precognitive events? I don't know. Maybe someday, precognitive events can be explained, at least conceptually, by physics' M-theory. Is it conceivable Riemannian manifolds from one membrane, a theory in physics that unifies all the consistent versions of superstring theory, can emerge momentarily in our observable three-dimensional space-time continuum? The whole subject is outside the scope of this book (and my education and experience). Maybe God plays pool with his parallel universes like He does with his galaxies in our observable universe. Why? Just for fun? Sometimes, maybe so. But then again, He may have a serious motive.

A Second Precognition

A few years later after a busy, long, but interesting business trip, I flew home from the East Coast on a late-afternoon flight. By the time I arrived at my apartment, I was tired. To my surprise, my fiancée opened the door before I could get my key in the lock. She had driven down from her home to spend the weekend. The moment I saw her face, I had the second direct precognitive event of my life. For no more than two seconds, her face melted away and all I saw was her skull. All I remember thinking to myself was *Whoa...* It seemed just like the highway sign experience a few years earlier. Did that mean something was going to happen to her in the next few days? What did it mean? I immediately asked God to not let anything happen to her.

I never said a word to my fiancée. I thought about the experience that night and the next day. I decided the experience was not a good sign. At that time in my life, I knew the power of asking God. Before my fiancée drove home on Sunday, I made sure I asked God a second time to intercede. Specifically, I asked Him to see that nothing happened to her. There was no surrender this time. If the Boss had approved the vision, I didn't need to surrender. Maybe I didn't need to do anything. Then again, maybe the highway sign experience was supposed to teach me about precognitive events and learn to ask. Namely, they may foretell a coming certain event that's part of the randomness of the God-human order—fate. Maybe asking is a crucial way to alter the future.

My fiancée and I married later that year. This year we will celebrate our twentieth anniversary. Since I have no clue how many years "a few years" might mean to the Boss, when my precious wife gets sick, I am very quick to act on any medical issue. My advice? If you experience a nontrivial precognitive event, know it is okay to ask God the event not occur. If precognitive events are not random, and I now don't believe they are, it's my judgment He wants us to ask. What do you have to lose by asking?

34. Other Precognitive Events

Ocean Shore Drive Premonition

Premonitions. We all have them. Most of us don't believe them until one comes along that really stuns us. Though I have had many, one stands out. After work on a warm summer afternoon, I decided to celebrate a particularly good day at work by taking a drive along the ocean. While I was taking the T-tops off my sports car, I was thinking about driving through a ninety-degree curve on the way to the ocean. I wanted to feel my car's multiple-point suspension hold the curve at a high rate of speed. Childish? Certainly.

As I approached the curve and started to pick up speed, I had a gut-wrenching sense something was seriously wrong. As I slowed down, I entered the curve below the speed limit. Good thing. An old blue Chevrolet pickup was stalled dead center in my lane. The truck was at the end of the curve—right in the blind spot. If I had not slowed down, I could not have stopped without running under the truck or off the road into a grove of large trees. It was the worst possible place for any vehicle to stall. Ever since this experience, I pay a lot of attention to premonitions. I often wondered if this premonition came from God or one of His angels. At least I reacted.

The premonition I had was different from intuition, fear, or the onset of common sense. It was very sudden and very loud. My response was somewhat panicky. When you have such a premonition, don't think about it. Just react. The consequences of not reacting may be serious!

Dreams

Everyone has dreams. Even my dog sometimes dreams he is running—maybe he was acting out his previous day's stresses. As one story goes, Crazy Horse, war leader of the Oglala Lakota Indian tribe, had a dream the Sioux encampment on the Little Bighorn River in Wyoming (1876) would be attacked by the US cavalry. Shortly after, it was attacked. Crazy Horse defeated Custer in the Battle. I wonder if Crazy Horse's dream story was true.

When I was young, I read a book on dreams. Wanting to test one of its hypotheses, I immediately made a mental note of a dream's details as soon as I woke the next morning. Apparently, remembering the dream's details as soon as we wake up is necessary since dream details fade quickly. At the end of the day, I realized I had, in fact, experienced the event exactly as I had dreamed. I know people who have had similar experiences.

Are some dreams another form of precognition? It's my judgment they are. I recommend paying attention to dreams that forebode something serious.

A Statue Story

One day, coming home from work, I had a sense one of my favorite possessions, a Wolf Runner Native American statue, had been broken. When I got home, my wife confessed she had accidentally broken the statue, which I then repaired. But it dawned on me—How did I sense the statue had been broken? Again, I remembered Albert Einstein said if the entropy (chaos) in the universe was not increasing, we could remember the future. Although one of my most obvious reality experiences, I was aware of this one in near real time. Some people might call such experiences just intuition or coincidence. Was Einstein correct, or did I sense the problem through some other means? Can we really remember or see the future in some way? How else can this experience be explained? The probability the experience was just coincidence is zero.

A Glowing Light

Early one morning two years ago, as I was entering my open garage, the whole garage and immediate outdoor area was lit up with a glowing yellow light. It lasted only a few seconds. I thought, *Wow, what was that all about?* As I sat at my garage coffee table with my morning coffee, I suddenly knew. As I went back into the house, I thanked God for telling me someday I would have enough money to survive and help others. With a thought, I told God, "If I have extra money, send others to me who need help." Later that very morning during a church service, a lady recently abandoned by her husband expressed her desperation over not being able to fix her plumbing problem. Had my wife not been going home to visit her family (a costly trip), I might have been able to help the lady without additional income. The two events of the day didn't seem coincidental. How and when would I have extra money? Lotto? This book? Maybe. I restarted working on this book after these two experiences so I can help people like this abandoned lady. A year later, we met another abandoned elderly lady who couldn't get caught up with her utility bills—we helped her.

35. What Is Precognition?

Precognition is awareness of a future event that actually occurs. Sometimes it's visual. Sometimes it's just intuitive. It is not just a psychic ability. Its basis is much more complex. It means the principle that "an effect cannot occur before its cause" is incorrect. That would require our four-dimensional space-time continuum be all that exists. It is not all that exists. M-theory (two-dimensional membranes) is not complete. Stephen Hawking suggested a search for a mathematical and physics theory of everything will never be complete. I wholeheartedly agree. Some things cannot be reduced to left-brain logical, rational, or prudent thinking.

I believe experienced reality, including precognition, might be understood as a superposition of many parallel universes, all created by God at one point in time—the big bang? Our ability to deduce our existence is due to dark matter does not preclude the existence of an intelligence beyond our *individual* ability to perceive it.

Personal experiences prove the existence of precognition (37 percent of Americans believe it exists). Personal experiences can also prove the existence of other realities—the existence of God, Satan, and the hereafter. For certain, in the face of experiencing precognition, our left brain's logical and rational way of thinking is trumped by our right brain's intuition and empathy.

VIII

Intuition

Intuition is a fundamental capacity of human reason to comprehend the true nature of reality.
—**Plato**

36. Work Experiences

Read

As I was reading through the Sunday paper many years ago, I was drawn to an article on the fewest moves it would take to win a chess game. Two days later during a work lunch break, I was challenged by the station's chess champion to play a game. As we started, he asked, "What color do you want?" Of course I knew to choose white—white moves first. He responded in probably the only manner required to ensure my win. We were both shocked. I then said "Well, I have to get back to work" and left the table. Afterwards, I felt bad. The way I left the table was rude. His pride was hurt. He would surely have won the second game. We never played again. Was it coincidence I read the paper and was drawn to the chess article? How and why was I drawn to it? I am not a good chess player. Was it God trying to increase my confidence or Satan trying to humiliate my friend? Or maybe a little of both? As I found out a few months later, apparently, I was supposed to continue reading the Sunday paper.

As a design division engineering manager, I had approved procurement of a critical real-time instrument controller. While I was touring the division's electronics laboratory, our best electronic design engineer was demonstrating why the new controller wasn't any faster than the old one. I had just read an article in the Sunday paper on why new computers might not perform faster than old ones—the screen updating algorithms often had not been or could not be updated to display as fast as the computers could process data. I suggested to the engineer he reduce the number of screen updates to a fraction of each test measurement loop and call me in my office to tell me the results. He did so. The new computer was much faster than the old one. Maybe the reason for the chess game incident was to motivate me to continue reading the local newspaper, thereby ensuring my design division's most critical projects would be completed on schedule. It may seem like a stretch, but not to me. Thank you, God.

With respect to reading, it is my understanding Muhammad went to a cave to talk to God. He apparently asked God, "I know you're here. What do you want me to do?" God literally said, "Read." Muhammad responded, "I don't know how to read. What else do you want me to do?" God again said, "Read." Apparently, they went through this cycle a total of four times. Anyone who literally hears the voice of God is a mystic. Clearly, Muhammad was a mystic. I think it's safe to say Muhammad learned to read. Based on my experiences, reading is one way God expects to communicate with us and indirectly to others. Why? The need to read is necessary to maintain free will. Reading gives us freedom, purpose, and guides us in making informed free will choices. The cool part? The resulting experiences are not coincidence.

Crane Manual

It was a tough project. The design engineering division I headed was responsible for getting three new range craft operational. When delivered to the Navy, most of the major shipboard systems did not meet our operational requirements. One system was particularly troublesome—the heavy lift cranes. Since they might someday lift weapons, they had to be certified to ordnance handling specifications. The cranes could not pass ordnance handling requirements. I assigned several teams to reverse engineer the crane subsystems.

From somewhere out of the blue, a copy of a Navy shipboard crane design document appeared on my desk. I didn't read it. After all, I had several teams working on the problem. They had copies of the document. I tossed the document in the trash can. The next morning when I came into work, the document was sitting in the center of my desk all by itself. *How did that get back on my desk?* I thought. This time I put the document into my file outbox; my secretary filed all such documents in the vault. There were many other documents in my file basket.

The next morning when I came into work, there was the crane document again in the center of my desk. Knowing we had serious crane problems, my secretary had put the document back on my desk with a note, "Did you want to read this before I filed it?" How did she know I hadn't read the document?

Well, I finally gave up and read the crane document. Holy heck. Our heavy lift cranes were squirt-boom cranes. Their basic design was not approved for ordnance handling. Once we realized our problem was much bigger than we thought, we redesigned most of the crane subsystems, tested the cranes to several times their maximum load, and certified the cranes for range use. The new systems met all our operational requirements for handling at least unmanned undersea vehicles.

This might seem like a small intervention, but it impacted several ten-million-dollar-plus projects. The impact was huge. When I got my job, I sensed God's hand. The lesson? If God points the way and helps you get there, He will help you every step of the way. You still must do the work—you must read the manual so you will know what you're doing.

Aid-to-Navigation (ATN) System Problem

Early in my career, I was fascinated by the advent of personal computers (PCs). I had programmed many mainframe and minicomputers in college and at work. I even had an opportunity to use a supercomputer. I was managing the development of a submarine aid-to-navigation (ATN) system that had been transferred from a research division to my design division. It did not work. I assigned a small group of engineers to determine the problem(s). They could not verify the cause. I had them evaluate the pulse width of the underwater received tracking signals. The report back was "the signals were normal." Compelled to get personally involved, I determined the received pulse widths were five milliseconds wider than they should have been, meaning two signals were overlapping. One had to be a reflection from the ocean bottom or surface. But which? Since time was critical, I took the data home and did a range simulation on my new PC. After two nights, I proved the problem was surface reflections that could only be compensated for by changing the tracking signal timing relative to the receiver locations. The redesigned range systems worked. Wow, I have been in love with PCs ever since. My position was at stake. But God was with me all the way, giving me the tools, intuition, and determination to find the problem and the solution. Coincidence? No way! Thank you again, God.

37. Opportunities Missed

Lotto Number Coincidences?

Many years ago, I had an interesting lotto experience. I had just read where a mega value (three hundred plus million dollar) winner said he was just drawn to the numbers. How could that be? Isn't winning the lotto just chance? So I tried to feel the numbers on a much smaller valued lotto game. I didn't feel anything. Since I was having trouble with my pen, I tried writing the same three numbers

(5, 6, and 7) I had used for decades to fix pen ink problems. As I was fixing the pen, the numbers 5, 6, and 9 came up! That didn't feel like coincidence, so I bought a lotto ticket with those three numbers. I just guessed at the last three numbers. Later that day as my wife and I were driving home from visiting family members, I wanted to tell her about the experience, but I didn't. The next morning, I checked the numbers, and sure enough, three of the numbers were 5, 6, and 9. None of my other three numbers came up.

Remembering back to the first lotto drawing twenty years earlier, I had also picked three matching numbers in the exact order they were drawn. What? But to top these experiences, two years after the first experience, I picked six lotto numbers but could not find the lotto ticket. Guess what. No one ever submitted the winning lotto ticket. These experiences don't seem like coincidence. If you have experiences like these, I hope you have better luck than I did. And keep track of your lotto tickets! It is better to know you didn't win than to wonder the rest of your life if you won and just carelessly lost the ticket. Did I lose the ticket, or did God have a hand in this experience? If he did, why? Time would answer my question. Maybe He didn't want me to be too comfortable and not do something hard like write a book or take on demanding projects.

Awareness Experiences Related to the Stock Market

The following items are examples of an intuitive sense of the future I could have capitalized on and didn't. Maybe God was somehow trying to help me survive some tough times. Life isn't just a gamble. He is with us trying to help without overriding our free will. I wish I had just gone with my intuition in the following examples.

2001 Experience. One June morning on the way to work, I asked God the question, "Should I move my retirement money to the stock market"? Immediately, the radio announced the market was up 350 points. So I took that as a sign and put my money into the stock market. Then 9/11 changed everything, at least for a short time. Yes, my stock account went down, but I stayed in and ended up okay. But what if I had waited until I had a buy sign like 9/11. Life is full of what-ifs. Be careful with signs. They may be only the first in a series.

Items needed by society. Over my work career in technology and being an overly enthusiastic consumer, I recognized many potentially significant opportunities like Intel's 4-bit microcontroller in the 1970s and Apple's cell phone in 2005 (a user-friendly device that didn't require an engineering degree to use). In 1987 when my brother-in-law passed away, my sister asked me where she should put some of his life insurance. I told her to put fifty thousand dollars into Microsoft stock, but her stock market analyst disagreed. If she had bought Microsoft and held it until December 1999, she might have made millions. But I didn't buy any Microsoft stock either, and I had the money to buy a small amount. In retrospect, these forecasts seem more like intuitive prophecies than mere guesses.

January 2008 forecast. In January 2008, the stock market and home values seemed overvalued. I did an estimate of where I thought the stock market would be by the end of the year and sent an email to my siblings warning about the potential for a significant stock mark drop. Of course no one believed me. The Dow Jones and Nasdaq indexes were slightly higher than I predicted by the end of 2008 but had fallen even lower earlier. One of my siblings lost a lot of money. The whole experience was strictly intuitive. Maybe it was a prophecy. Did I buy index put options? Of course not—I didn't have the courage. Early the following year, I read an article that suggested "the book to value" accounting requirement be removed. When that was done, the market recovered. Amazon stock had dropped significantly during the crash—it seemed like a buy. Again, too bad I didn't buy any. The stock recently closed up forty times since the 2008 crash. Why didn't I follow my intuition? No courage and fear of losing the little I had. When you feel something is going to happen, act. Do it in moderation. You don't have to bet the farm. It is my judgment this forecast was really a prophecy.

AWARE OF THE ULTIMATE REALITY

38. A Glimpse of the Hereafter from Science?

So where are God, heaven, and hell? Can we find physical evidence of anything? Anywhere? Science has some evidence of hypothetical dark matter, dark energy, and dark flow. What do they mean by "dark"? Per Wikipedia, Dark matter is a theorized form of matter that may account for 80 percent of the

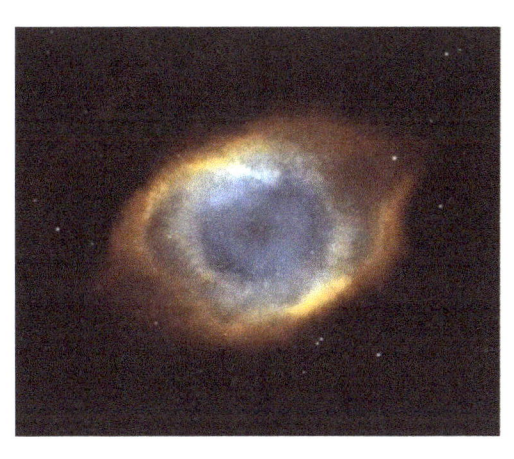

The Eye of God (NASA Picture)

mass-energy in our observable universe. Dark energy is theorized to permeate all of space, tending to accelerate expansion of the universe. Dark flow is theorized to account for the nonrandom peculiar velocity of galaxies. There may be many anisotropic (different properties in different directions) multiverses or parallel universes. In my opinion, the issue may be supported in some manner by analysis of the cosmic microwave background (CMB) with its many black/dark spots, by observing super galactic collisions, and, I am sure, other areas of investigation. I leave the whole subject to astrophysics. It's not the subject of this book. Or is it?

It's my judgment anyone can prove, at least to oneself, there are interactions in our individual lives that defy society's logical way of understanding reality. Is it logical, rational, and/or prudent to assume other realities exist? Imagine a person who has heard the voice of God, the voice of a deceased parent, the voice of Satan, experienced direct interventions, divine interactions, and experienced answered asks all related to his or her life in the here and now. Wouldn't such a person have a completely unique awareness of the ultimate reality? Of course. Experiences such as those couldn't occur without the existence of an ultimate reality, existing beyond our directly observable everyday life. Parallel universes and/or dark matter would have to be part of such an ultimate reality. Some authorities say we owe our very existence to dark matter. And I add, to God.

39. What Is Intuition?

According to Wikipedia (en.wikipedia.org/wiki/Intuition), *intuition* is the ability to acquire knowledge without proof, evidence, or conscious reasoning without understanding how the knowledge was acquired. Different writers give the word *intuition* a variety of different meanings, ranging from direct access to unconscious knowledge, unconscious cognition, inner sensing, inner insight to unconscious pattern-recognition, and the ability to understand something instinctively, without the need for conscious reasoning. In the East, intuition is mostly entwined with religion and spirituality. In the West, intuition does not appear as a separate field of study (see Wikipedia).

One nineteenth-century psychologist believed knowledge could only be attained through intellectual manipulation of carefully made observations and rejected any other means of acquiring knowledge such as intuition. In other words, knowledge could be gained only by logical, rational thinking. Another psychologist defined *intuition* as "perception via the unconscious." He speculated that humans experience the world using four principal psychological functions—sensation, intuition, feeling, and thinking. Personally, I believe the second psychologist's definition is more correct than the first psychologist's view. Then again, maybe they are both wrong. Don't overthink reality and don't assume an expert's view is correct. Appeal to authority is a logical fallacy. There is only one ultimate reality. Feel and sense it for yourself.

An Islandic concept (InnSaei) enabling humans to connect through empathy and intuition is interesting. In their view, decisions, at the highest level, are intuitive. Intuitive, right-brained people seem to learn over time, processing everything going on around them. We all have the ability (barring head injuries) to function with both our logical, rational mind (left brain) and our intuitive/empathetic mind (right brain). It's my judgment becoming aware of the ultimate reality requires use of both sides of our brain. It is also my observation some people with narrow, logical, rational views of life do not want to change. They may never appreciate the importance of intuition. From my perspective, the experiences of my life cannot be dismissed. My experiences are as real as it gets! I go with Plato's view on intuition.

IX

This Book

40. Why Write the Book?

The awareness I had a book to write first occurred when I was nineteen during a conversation with my mother. Her comment? "It sounds like you want to start a new religion." I responded, "The world has thousands of orthodox religions. It doesn't need another one. If there is an ultimate reality, any book I write will speak to a personal relationship between God and oneself." My mother occasionally read me poems as I was growing up. One, "Invictus" by William Henley, attached to the end of this book, often comes to mind: "I am the master of my fate, I am the captain of my soul." Being aware definitely affects one's fate and soul.

In 1995 I had a second serious hernia operation. I was out of commission for several weeks. During my recovery, I turned on the last five minutes of a TV show where the host was discussing a best-selling author's current book—I didn't know the title; I tuned in too late. The host asked the author what he thought would be the best book of all time. He outlined a book summarizing a person's life experiences similar to experiences in the holy books. The host said, "You're a good writer. Why don't you write it?" The author responded, "I haven't had those kinds of experiences." When the show ended, I thought about what the author said. I realized I had many of those kinds of experiences. I speculated whether or not the Boss put me through the suffering of major surgery so I would hear this interview.

It's my judgment that the whole experience was not coincidence. Why didn't I start the book then? I was too busy working and taking care of young children. But I should have started keeping a diary.

After experiencing God's voice in the late 1980s asking me to live—fall in love, write a book, and be passionate about something—I knew someday I would have to write a book based on experiences that expressed my passion and love of His beautiful world with all its varied cultures, children, animals, and curious creatures. On second thought, maybe I wasn't supposed to write the book until now. I have had my greatest experiences interacting with the ultimately reality in the last fifteen years. I have learned what it means to see the world through God's eyes, sense His presence, and share His feelings. I know why the twelve disciples and St. Paul gave their lives to God and Jesus. Why? So you and I would also know there is an omnipresent loving and caring God.

Over a decade ago while I was dressing for the day, I again asked God if he still wanted me to write this book—"After all, who cares? Who would read it?" The events the rest of that day were not coincidence. As I was cutting weeds later in my backyard, a weed eater head bolt fell out. After looking for it without success, I decided to just buy a new head. As I drove into the yard-equipment business's parking lot, I noticed a Christian bookstore across the street that also served coffee. A group of seniors were listening to two young men very passionately discussing their views on religion, including the power of asking. As my coffee was being made, I went over and put my arm around one of the young men and told everyone at the table, "This young man is correct." I added a few words of my own, got my coffee, a new weed eater head, and went home to finish my yardwork. As I was restarting my weed eater in the backyard, I saw the missing head bolt in plain sight! There is no way I could have missed seeing the bolt. Can God keep us from seeing something that's right in front of us? Did He prevent me from seeing the bolt so I would have to go down to the store to witness the Bible study group and the two intense young men? By doing so, did he not answer my question about *who cares? Who would read such a book?* Did I see the bolt only after I returned so I would know He did it deliberately? It is my judgment He directed the whole experience.

Recently, I woke up one morning asking God why this book was so important to Him. This is what He put into my mind.

> *In the end, He is. Humanity can hear Him, see Him, and talk to Him every day! We don't need to be lectured, warned, or threatened by others. Once we are aware, we only need to do so willingly out of love for Him and his creation. This pull does not negate our free will. It is important that we individually decide and act accordingly. We need not be victims of orthodox dictatorships—someone else telling us what is true and how to be. God is not telling you what to think or believe—just follow your heart. Once you are aware, you don't need experts or authorities to tell you how to live. You will just know.*

There were many other experiences that encouraged me, even directed me to write this book, not for myself, but for Him and for you, the reader.

41. Distractions

I should have expected the Boss to use distractions in my life while I was writing this book. He tried. First, through a writer's strike, he cancelled all the prime-time television shows I really enjoyed watching. That didn't seem like coincidence. But a couple of other distractions were even subtler.

One Friday night, when my wife was visiting relatives in her home country, I went to the grocery store to get dinner and staples for the following week. As I walked into the store, I stopped at the DVD movie machine. When it was my turn, I tried renting two movies I had been looking forward to seeing. I had used the machine several times over the last year. However, this time I could not check out the movies. Every time I went to the cart to pay, the machine hung. I couldn't get it to work. The lady behind me asked if I needed help. I said, "No, I think I already have Someone helping me." She must have thought I was nuts. Suddenly I knew I wasn't supposed to waste a night.

The next morning, I got up early and tried to get my music organized for the next month. I got all the CD cartridges arranged the way I wanted. Unfortunately, it took a couple of hours. I loaded the first cartridge into the CD player. It wouldn't play. I cleaned the laser head with no luck. So there I was with no TV, no movies, and no CD player. What other distraction did I have? I couldn't think of anything else to do, so I started doing the reading research I wanted to do for the book. No more excuses. I knew I had to write the book.

Ten years ago, I received an interesting email from a friend. He knew I was writing a spiritual book, so he sent me a four-page email describing his most dramatic spiritual event. I sent back a quick email telling him I found his experience very interesting. I asked him some questions, and he responded with a brief email.

For some reason, I had the sense I needed to just write my book, at least through the first draft, without collaborating with anyone, including friends. Too bad I didn't heed that sense. As I went to call him, the power was out on my phone. My first thought was I shouldn't call him. It felt like God was deliberately distracting me. I thought, *That's nuts*. It took me about twenty minutes to fix the problem. The phone had come unplugged. It had never happened before and has not happened since. After I fixed the phone, I went to call a second time. Someone rang the doorbell. It turned out to be the UPS driver with a delivery. I opened and checked the package, which took another ten minutes. As I was reaching for the phone to call my friend for the third time, the phone rang almost in my hand. It was one of my sons. We talked for almost half an hour.

After the phone call, I seriously questioned all the interruptions. Maybe the Boss didn't want me to call my friend. But for what reason? I wasn't interrupted when I made the fourth attempt to call. Wow, do I wish I had been. We discussed a few of the book's general themes. He immediately told me, "Everyone knows God doesn't do those kinds of interventions." As far as he was concerned, his experiences were real; mine weren't. I got off the phone as soon as I could. I found myself questioning what I was doing and why.

A day later, I recovered my motivation by remembering all the distractions from God, including His interventions in trying to keep me from making the call to my friend in the first place. I finally realized the Boss wanted me to write this book with just *His* help. The fact that my friend didn't concur with the asking premise was something I should have expected. The message? Always be aware of God's helping hand and respond accordingly. After this whole experience, I was again highly motivated with a newfound awareness of His presence.

Much later a new distraction arose. Taking on subjects like those in this book, especially with miracles and the emphasis on direct interactions with God, is bound to be criticized by many where subjects like religion, intuition, and so forth threaten those with laissez-faire views (the practice or doctrine of noninterference in the affairs of others, especially with reference to individual conduct or freedom of action). History shows those who fear change and any judgment of their lifestyle will literally crucify bearers of "the good news." The history of St. Paul the apostle, Jesus's twelve disciples, and all the saints bear this out, at least to some degree.

When I was shaving one morning with a new multibladed razor and contemplating the possible negative consequences of writing this book, I suddenly cut my lower chin so badly I couldn't completely stop the bleeding for the better part of two days. I never had an experience like that before and haven't had one since. It's my judgment the experience was not just coincidence. I wasn't supposed to be distracted by worrying about the possible negative consequences of finishing this book. Once I realized what had happened and why, I remained determined to finish this book, whatever the personal consequences.

42. An Ask Answered

When I first got up one morning after just starting the book, I reviewed the first five pages. They didn't excite me. One of my sons visited just after I had finished a rough draft of the first chapter. Moments before my son drove up, I had asked God to *tell me how I was doing in no uncertain terms. And please do so literally.* As my son came in the house, I thought I would show him the book's first page. He critiqued it rather harshly. How did my son come to those conclusions after having read only one page? Had God answered my question through my son? Not only was I told the style to use and how it should read but also the incremental phases needed to finish the book. Was the information useful? Was it correct? Absolutely. I never deviated from God's direction provided *literally* via my son. Apparently, God can put thoughts and words into someone's mind and compel the person to relay the information to you without them even being aware they are doing so. Pay attention to what you ask for. If He decides to answer your ask, accept the results. The original first chapter is no longer a part of this book per God's direction provided via my son.

43. Wave of a Hand

Some things seem unbelievable to me. Once when I was alone well over a decade ago, I went to my backyard to ponder writing this book. Just as I exited the house, a neighbor started his lawnmower. I couldn't think. In an angry mood, I turned in the neighbor's direction, several houses away, waved my hand in the direction of the noise, willing the mower shut off. It shut off and stayed off. Another time a car repair facility wanted to charge me a lot of money to fix a problem. I couldn't do it. The next morning, the door locks were still turning on and off, discharging my battery. Again, I waved the back of my hand at the car, willing the problem cease. It did—and did not return. If at a given moment, when we are in a high state-of-grace and doing what He wants done, can we will something to happen and have it actually happen? If you have surrendered to God's will, maybe. Were these two events meant to distract me from working on this book? The car problem distracted me for over a week. Were these distractions Satan's doing? Most likely.

44. The Rule of Thirds?

While I was writing this book, a curious thought crossed my mind. I call it the rule of thirds. Hitler came to power with only one-third of the German people supporting him. Only one-third of the American population supported the revolution; one-third were loyalists supporting the king of England, and one-third were indifferent. The ratio holds true for those who believe in precognition. Maybe one-third don't believe in precognition and one-third don't care? Maybe the rule holds true to some degree for all human endeavors. If valid, is it a natural consequence of free will and therefore proof of an ultimate reality consisting of good, evil, and indifference? Does it matter to us at an individual level? I suggest it's even more reason to develop an ethos (charter, ethics) that actively seeks caring behavior. Are fame and fortune irrelevant pursuits? Material things—superficial? What if we make agape love and compassion for the sick, suffering, and needy our all-consuming motive? If we take the high road, will we hear the voice of God, share His feelings, and have Him respond to our asks? Based on my experiences, I believe so.

X

Final Remarks

Awareness isn't the end. It's the beginning.

As a lady once told me, faith starts with belief. For some that is sufficient. But it's my view becoming aware is the next step. Awareness results in knowing. What does it take to know? By learning to recognize precognitive events, miracles, direct interventions, divine interactions, and sensing God's presence or feelings (and, if necessary, hearing God's and/or Satan's voice). You will know God, heaven, and Satan are real. And forevermore, you will be aware. You learn God communicates daily through feelings and intuition. You end up knowing what God is thinking and feeling. You no longer need the Voice. The reward? Seeing creation through His loving eyes. You will feel His love for all others (children, the ill, the handicapped, the homeless, the elderly, and all cultures and races), all animals, and the beautiful home he has given us with its mountains, rivers, oceans, and plains.

You will feel His sorrow for those who choose not to know Him. When you encounter a lost soul, *ask* God to help them become aware and/or prevent them from harming others. Provide God with your justification as to why you're asking; it doesn't necessarily have to be done by thoughts, though that helps. It's your feelings you share with him. Asking and forgiving seem to free Him to act outside any "free will" limitations. Your asking may be the only way a lost soul will ever be changed or, if necessary, removed.

Remember what Shakespeare said, "Love all, trust a few, do wrong to none." I suspect anyone who does not share Shakespeare's view is at risk of being influenced by Satan—the essence of selfishness, hate, jealousy, exaggerated pride, flat-out murder, and destruction of God's creations. Defend yourself, family, community, nation, culture, and all humanity against evil—regardless of the personal costs. You can always ask God for His help, His guidance, and, if necessary, His direct intervention.

God asked me to live (fall in love, be passionate about something, and write a book). What He wants you to do will likely be different. Determine and focus on your purpose(s), your talents, and respect God's gifts to you (children, family, friends, and animals). Share His love by respecting everyone. Help the poor and needy. Enjoy every moment of every day. Listen to music, read, walk, camp out, work in a garden, play with a child, pet an animal, paint, hike, ride a bike—whatever gives you joy. Thank God every day for being with you. If God compels you to talk to a complete strange, even if it is just to say "good morning," do it. If they seem irritated or don't answer back, do it anyway.

God *is* with you and your family every moment of every day. Believe it. No matter how hard life seems at times, welcome Him into your life. By respecting and helping others the best you can, you are respecting and helping God. Teach your children this reality so they also can become aware. "We cannot change the cards we are dealt, just how we play the hand" (Randy Pausch, *The Last Lecture*). The *ask* card is in all our hands.

The Unexpected Alarm

A short time ago, I was very tired but went to bed at the usual time. I needed to get up early to review the final draft of this book. We didn't have any alarms set. Suddenly, near 6:00 a.m., I heard a very loud alarm go off. I quickly sat up and asked my wife if she set her alarm. She said no. She didn't hear an alarm. We had no cell phones or telephones in the bedroom. I suddenly realized, even though I hadn't literally heard His voice in years, I knew the alarm was His doing. I immediately got up, took our elderly dog out to do his business, and got right to work on finishing this book. We may not know how He is going to communicate with us, but be assured He will wake us up. He is gentle but determined. Later that morning, I knew the alarm was good news for this book. He really wanted it done. No more too tired or lazy, I had a job to do—for Him and for you. So take this book seriously. Apparently, He does.

Interesting Quotes

> To live is to suffer; to survive is to find meaning in the suffering. (Viktor E. Frankl)

> Success, like happiness, cannot be pursued (if you aim at it you're going to miss); it must ensue, and it only does so as ***the unintended side-effect of one's personal dedication to a cause greater then oneself…*** Happiness must happen, and the same holds for success: you must let it happen by caring about it. (Viktor E. Frankl)

> Abundance of evidence is not the same as evidence of absence. (Carl Sagan)

> Even if you're not aware, He is always there. (J. R. Morris)

> Agape love, the virtue of charity, surpasses all other kinds of love. Agape love is patient and always kind. It never fails. It rises above everything (based on a Saint Paul quote).

ATTACHMENT 1
(From Wikipedia)

When I was ten years old, the following was one of the first poems my mother read to me. A seed planted that started me thinking about life experiences? I think so.

Invictus
By William E. Henley

Out of the night that covers me,
Black as the pit from pole to pole,
I thank whatever gods may be
For my unconquerable soul.

In the fell clutch of circumstance
I have not winced nor cried aloud.
Under the bludgeonings of chance
My head is bloody, but unbowed.

Beyond this place of wrath and tears
Looms but the Horror of the shade,
And yet the menace of the years
Finds, and shall find me, unafraid.

It matters not how strait the gate,
How charged with punishments the scroll,
I am the master of my fate,
I am the captain of my soul.

The fourth stanza alludes to a phrase from the King James Bible, which has, at Matthew 7:14, "Because strait is the gate, and narrow is the way, which leadeth unto life, and few there be that find it." This poem seems to answer how the author dealt with his health problems. The last two lines seem to suggest his acceptance of free will.

About the Author

The author has three degrees in physics, engineering, and management—two at the graduate level, earning membership in a National Honor Society. His experience covers over twenty years as a senior manager leading development of high priority defense department projects. He made significant contributions resulting in two meritorious unit awards. One was the first Military Meritorious Unit Award ever awarded to a civilian unit. In his defense department civilian positions and as head of research and technology development at a major university physics laboratory, he had frequent interactions with senatorial and congressional representatives, senior Department of Defense officials, and senior contractor managers. Formal presentations contributed to major defense department acquisition decisions. He personally solved several serious underwater system design problems, led development of a patented new type of head-mounted display, and started a local Boy Scout Explorer Post in computer science.